# THE POSSIBILITIES OF POTENTIAL

SHALINI KAMBOJ
SAMEER KAMBOJ

*Narration by Gayatri Manchanda*

To my mother, Chander Prabha, who encouraged me to explore life and become who I am, and for not making me who she thought I should be.

-Sameer Kamboj

To an unseen Grace, which helped me sail through life as a journey filled with amazing and enlightening experiences.

-Shalini Kamboj

First Edition: 2016
Second Edition: 2017

Disclaimer: This is a work of fiction. Names, characters, businesses, places, events and incidents are either the products of the authors' imaginations or used in a fictitious manner. Any resemblance to actual persons, living or dead, or actual events is purely coincidental.

ISBN: 978-81-940561-0-2

Published by
SKC Consulting Private Limited
Add: F-26/3, Second Floor,
Okhla Industrial Area, Phase-2
New Delhi-110020

Printed by
Color Dots Prepress Studio
Add: 208, 2nd Floor, DSIDC She,
Okhla Industrial Area, Phase-1
New Delhi-110020

# ACKNOWLEDGEMENT————————————

We would like to acknowledge Gayatri Manchanda, who worked tirelessly with us to make this book a reality. She sat with us for hours, understood us, and wrote with us. Thank you, Gayatri.

We would also like to acknowledge our silent and patient son, Vidit, who has always believed in us and for years lived with the hope that we would one day reach out to a wider audience through the medium of a book. His faith and belief in us makes us stronger.

We would like to thank Abhinand Shankar who did multiple rounds of editing and proof reading. A young boy, so talented and willing, that we are lucky to know him.

We would like to acknowledge those participants and people we have mentored over these years who have stood by us and used our offerings to improve their lives.

We would like to make a special mention of Chaitanya, our partner who is also like a son to us, without whom we would not have found the time to bring this book to all of you.

-Shalini & Sameer Kamboj

# CONTENTS

# PROLOGUE

Goals are directions, enabling people to retain their focus. Many goal-setting theories introduced through the years have supposedly helped mankind fulfil their quest for greater achievement. The world has indeed progressed and the previous 100 years have witnessed more progress than what was achieved over 10 centuries. However, this idea of progress, according to many, is debatable – for humans today suffer more than ever.

Certain cultures speak of their golden past, an age where people were both happy and prosperous. When studying these times, we find that the accounts of these pasts demonstrate an emerging and evolutionary state in the people's consciousness, where they had scientifically researched the source of human joy and happiness.

Over the ages, the purpose of most studies, thinking and research has been to find ways to accomplish progress and success that also brings in a sense of fulfilment. While some people found answers that worked for them as individuals or as a group of people, the task of making these solutions applicable to larger sections of people continued to remain a challenge. In common parlance, those who did find such solutions were considered wise, while those who could help others find such answers were considered Masters.

*

Desires define us, motivate us, push us, force us to act, and propel us to never ever give up. Yet, we want to run away from our desires as they haunt us, and at times ask us to become who and what we are not. While some say that running after desires and abandoning them mid-way produces suffering, many others profess that desires must be nurtured in moderation to avoid suffering. Talk of contentment and satisfaction do the rounds mostly because our understanding of desires has been confusing, to say the least.

We have found ourselves trying to make either one of two decisions—

1.      Give up all desires.

2.      Desire in moderation.

The answer to both decisions – based on our experiences with ourselves and countless other people – is an emphatic "No".

Through our insights and experiences, we realized that desires were a founding source of human conflict, both internally and externally. Thus a better understanding of our desires would be the key to unlocking the answer to a journey of fulfilment.

In more than 20 years of our active engagement with people from all walks of life, we realized that there is another fundamental human conflict that lies in our hearts. This conflict deals with the awareness of a limitless potential that exists in each of us, even though we only possess a vague idea about the manner in which this potential can be actualised in our living reality. This conflict is seen to arise with greater degree in people at the higher echelons of society. This means that education, or motivation, or even success does not really empower people to resolve this fundamental conflict of our untapped Potential with the tapped Potential.

*

*The Possibilities of Potential* is an attempt to provide an answer to the quest of unlimited, conflicting, and fathomless desires, which lie submerged in our limitless potential, awaiting an exploration of countless possibilities. This book deals with both of these interwoven conflicts (of desires and potential) that create the confounding mystery called life.

Our active engagements seem to have a magical impact on people, many of whom have resolved this conflict with great ease and elan. We developed and used a tool to aid this process. As a result of feedback from hundreds of people urging us to disseminate this concept, we have decided to offer our learning and experience to you – the wider audience.

This is our humble offering of an understanding, methodology, and technique that will provide you with the answer to the riddle that life confronts us with at all times. Please accept this offering and explore its application and significance in your life. This offering is neither a theory, nor a philosophy. It is a simple and clever process that gives you your answers, every time. We silently pray and wish that each reader start a journey of awareness and clarity about their desires, and embrace them as possibilities awaiting exploration and actualization through the harnessing of their potential.

# THE TRAVEL

My air tickets, the travel arrangements to USA, and travelling itself did not prove much of a challenge to me. Having travelled across continents, I can easily become a travel guru and help people step out of their comfort zones and explore the real world, beyond the virtual one of the World Wide Web.

The car glided on the neon-lit National Highway 8 on the outskirts of New Delhi*. It could have been any city of the world at this hour but the sweet smell of the wet earth from amongst the shrubs planted along the road divider reminded me that I was still on the home turf, and that it was Spring! It was still four hours to the scheduled take-off, but I liked to be early for my flight. I loved to witness the different world that thrived at the airports. It was a place that had an uncanny resemblance to a resting space, where people transitioned between their journeys to specific destinations. Some may say it is the same like life on Earth, before you find your final destination. It used to be better earlier when people did not keep themselves distracted with their mobile devices. It was quite different now, yet I still enjoyed the experience.

The US tour was one I had been looking forward to for some time. Many deep thinkers were to attend this conference where I was to speak. Most participants, I had been informed, belonged to the entrepreneurial and business community. In spite of explaining to the organisers that I did not really like to "just speak", they still wanted me to do that. If only preaching could solve all the issues, then this world would be a different place to live in. For better or worse, we really cannot say.

However, what they did not know was that my plan entailed doing something that I loved to do during such speaking engagements, which made them different.

*

One of the big joys of travelling is meeting new people and interacting with them. People who are happy to share their victories and success stories have the courage to reflect upon failures and challenges in overcoming defeat, who bare their innermost desires and seek answers from strangers.

Human beings are forever aiming at bringing stability, growth, or expansion in their lives. In many cases, they are unable to achieve what they aspire for because of their own doing. Once they themselves stop being a bottleneck, stability sets in and they start to grow. To be growth-driven, one needs to know not just one's mind but oneself, all the while remaining open to all kinds of possibilities.

The car slowed down and we had reached the airport. Even at midnight, the Indira Gandhi International Airport looked as busy as the New Delhi Railway Station. People with a lot of luggage were swarming around all the counters while I entered the airport with my relatively scanty luggage and quickly checked in. Stealing a glance at the shining brass hands in a lotus position decorating the sparkling lobby, I moved towards the immigration counter.

The uniformed, pleasant-looking, middle-aged officer there looked at me through a pair of thick-rimmed glasses that threatened to slide down the bridge of his nose.

 "So, you are a speaker at the International Leadership Seminar at Boston," he said.

I have the habit of showing the invitations for my journeys at the immigration counters, as it pleases the officers to know more and adds to their comfort level. I smiled and nodded. He smiled back and handed me my passport with folded* hands.

**2**

# REQUEST

The journey was long, but enriching and restful. I was both well-fed and undisturbed. My practices kept me centred and engaged within my being during the air travel. Thankfully, it was a direct flight, avoiding the trouble of me being in transit once again. When we arrived at Boston, my co-travellers slowly moved out of the aircraft towards the arrivals to collect their baggage. Jet lag was distinctly visible on most of their faces. I wanted to reach out to them to let them know about a way to remain completely fresh during long-haul flights.

*Amazing possibilities are offered by the Indian system of Yoga*, which still remained unexplored.*

The restlessness and anxiety I had observed on many faces at the time of boarding the flight at New Delhi had disappeared. An eerie sense of calmness prevailed instead. After all, we were approaching the US immigration counters. My paperwork helped me again and the well-armed officer at the counter gave me a friendly and courteous welcome.

People hugged their loved ones as they exited from the airport and a feeling of bonhomie engulfed the atmosphere while I looked for a placard stating my name.

*How do our names become our identity in a world of strangers? Do people face identity crises when they meet their namesakes? The vagaries of a wandering mind would never leave you alone unless you knew how to deal with yourself and keep yourself above the mind.*

The hotel where my stay was organized was going to be my home for the next five days. This annual conference had become a sought-after destination for thinkers and leaders from across the globe. I had successfully evaded it for years but was perhaps destined to attend it and that too with a talk. I felt like such a misfit amongst all the learned people, but my domain, consisting largely of contemplation and insights, could perhaps throw a different light.

After checking into my room, I stepped out into the balcony to take in the sight of the beautiful trees in the public garden. There was a nip in the air and the pores on my arm tingled at the thought of exploring a new city. It was still some time before daylight faded, and the idea of roaming around the place before a quick dinner seemed worthwhile. The conference would not start until 9am the next day. I also planned to walk around the Boston Common and Faneuil Hall in the early morning to acclimatize the mind and sensory organs to the freshness of a new city.

Each city adds something by breaking a bit into us. One carries back some part of each city s/he has the fortune of visiting. Places play an important role in our evolution. Travel makes people transcend the psychological realities they live in. It expands the mind and forces us to seek answers. It offers an opportunity to witness ways of living other than the one we are accustomed to. It rarely provides answers and that is the best thing.

A stay for two more days in Boston after the three day conference would give me enough time to meet a few new people who would be interested in what I had to offer. Wise ones always know how to seek when they find a source.

*

Another event planned as a part of this tour was a few days, perhaps a week, spent with an Indian family who had invited me to stay with them. Well-known in their community, this family had business interests both in India and USA. They had started their journey in India and now they all lived together in New York. The family was regarded as an aggressive and ambitious one, making its mark on the global business map. Yet, their invitation intrigued me.

This invite, one that I could not refuse, was more of an affectionate command hinting at urgency, rather than a request. I had come to learn that the definition of being "successful" was a source of misery for them now. My distinguished acquaintance from New Delhi, who had been an old friend of the founder and patriarch of the family, had tried to give me certain details and had also provided me with a file on them. However, I liked to meet people with an uncluttered mind – a blank slate. On the bright side, since they were in the hospitality business, staying with this family would guarantee me some good food.

# AUDIENCE

High profile conferences work on the same theme and offer the same experience.

A certain section of the audience comprises of people with the mindset of tourists, who tend to explore and collect knowledge as souvenirs to be displayed later. Another section of people is "unwilling", comprising of those who are already full. For them, these conferences serve little purpose, for they are either gracing the event or obliging someone. But for them, personally, it is a waste of time. A small section consists of people who are "willing". They are curious, eager, and progressive in a way that is self-destructive, wherein they are willing to shake loose their previously held notions. They are "explorers". I was hoping to meet a few of them this time.

Speaking for myself, I expected to learn from some of the amazing speakers and participants. I could clearly see the synergy each one brought to the three-day conference. There were some eager faces sitting around the tables in the large hall, mostly clad in business suits and shining neckties. I was reminded of my first job that I couldn't simply continue doing, due to the compulsion of wearing a necktie. Event managers perhaps knew of the dominance of dark suits and had accordingly used a theme of light grey and sky blue, to symbolize clear skies and a calm ocean.

As the conference progressed, I could sense a clear shift in the primary motivators, who moved their vision from money to meaning. Discussions on the virtues of the wider reach of spirituality, the use of digital media and of social entrepreneurship made the rounds.  These made their mark on new and young entrepreneurs seeking the real purpose of living. A lot of data on human needs research showed that Maslow's hierarchy of needs was certainly being questioned by the new generation. Even those at lower hierarchical levels were, in rising magnitude, seeking meaning along with money. It seemed like a step towards evolution.

In one session discussing the "barriers to growth of the human race", I learnt of some astonishing statistics on the healthcare (and pharmaceutical) industry being on the verge of surpassing the largest industry on the planet, the food industry! This was an amazing insight into two aspects of a changing paradigm where (a) health is becoming a priority for all stakeholders like individuals, industries, and governments and (b) how people have begun designing unhealthy lifestyles. The amount of money spent on food would soon be lower than the amount of money spent on medicines and healthcare in the near future. It surely was an indicator of the ill health of the masses. The most surprising statistics revealed that the bulk of this money was being spent on managing and treating emotional and psychological disorders. The fear of this malady turning into an epidemic loomed largely over the world.

Many speakers at the conference talked about how people

and industries have far more potential than what is being currently applied. Human potential remained one of the most under-utilised resources on the planet! When pitted against the healthcare expenditure of people, it was evident that underutilization of potential is both the cause as well as the effect of this imbalanced healthcare expense.

*

My talk towards the end of Day 2 was the main attraction at the conference. Day 2 was the last full day of the Conference, after which the Gala dinner was planned. The morning of Day 3 witnessed the closing of the conference, discussions on the agenda for next year's conference, and ended with people proceeding with their Spring-break plans.

Many participants had expressed their curiosity towards my session and had heard that I was mostly spontaneous and spoke extempore to meet the needs of the audience. But then that was true for my closed group sessions. I rarely "just spoke" for a large audience. There were some wet eyes and I could hear a sniff or two towards the end of the session as I talked about the root cause of unexplored potential and time lost in our lives just 'thinking' about life while missing out on opportunities to participate in it. There was a brief, intense silence after the applause. Then, many questions later, we dispersed.

Post the conference there were several questions from many attendees. People were intrigued to hear of the possibilities to increase their potential without an external intervention in the long run. Appointments were confirmed for the next two days and I received an invite from the eminent professors of Harvard University to visit them the following day. After setting the agenda for the next day, I stepped out to visit the public gardens and to spend some time reflecting in solitude on new avenues as I walked on a well-trodden path.

I explored Boston city further, post each session of the conference, interacting with people on the street and at the places I visited. Evenings at the hotel were spent in the company of other speakers, sharing insights and new theories. A sea of exchange of thoughts and ideas took place at the dinner table amidst frowns, smiles and the laughter of intellectuals from across the globe.

I gave some thought to the next leg of my journey, which would present me with unknown challenges. These challenges would require me to help find solutions to issues that raised their heads and created a debilitating effect on most families and businesses. My answers to those challenges would not be enough. The real challenge would be to help the family and its members find their answers from within.

# 4

# THE FAMILY

PS was able to get me a seamlessly smooth checkout and a warm farewell from the hotel. I realized it helped being a well-known hotelier with apparently amazing connections in the fraternity. While placing my luggage in the boot of his silver Cadillac convertible, he looked surprised to see my scanty luggage for a nearly two-week-long overseas trip but said nothing. He opened the passenger seat door politely and moved towards the driver's side. I was set for my journey, this time to New York.

"Uncle Yuri spoke very highly of you. You must be an amazing man to have him hold you in such high regard. He is not an easy man to please!" PS chuckled, perhaps with a memory of a childhood prank gone wrong, thus breaking the long silence that had lingered between us since we left Boston.

It was my turn to speak. I asked, "PS, is that your real name?" I find abbreviations intriguing.

He laughed and said, "No sir, it is Shekhar Punj. PS is what my friends call me. Family name first, as if it is my sole identity!"

Did that seem like a mix of pride and sorrow? Maybe that was a hint.

A twist of his left wrist revealed a tiny tattoo hidden in the folds of his wrist lines. He said, "See what they made me do. Tattoo my life-long dream on my wrist during our last mountaineering trip."

"Tiny but beautiful," I said, with a smile.

"Yes," PS replied sheepishly, a boyish grin rising behind his shy demeanour.

After a brief pause, he continued. "My family wouldn't approve of it though, my wife included. She comes from a traditional Indian family. We've just been married, and so I am not sure how well she will take to my unconventional outlook towards life. I have a contrarian view on everything that is the seemingly acceptable societal norm for success.

"When I am not climbing mountains, I watch Indian plays or play the violin with other music aficionados. The office doesn't need much of my presence. I have a wonderful team that holds the fort for me at work."

He paused, and then said, smiling with excitement, "By the way, I have another tattoo. Would you like to see?"

I nodded and he turned his head around. A small trishul* was neatly engraved on his nape.

"I must have scaled all the mountain ranges of the East and West coasts of USA, some in Canada and Alaska but my ultimate dream is to scale a few in the mighty Himalayas, visit Kailash Mansarovar* and spend a month at Darchin and Dirapuk near Kailash. I wonder if I can ever go there though," he stated wistfully, his eyes fixed somewhere far beyond the confines of the car.

"Why not?"

My question was met with an impassive silence.

*

It was Spring, and the journey was pleasant on the country roads. With multihued flowers and leaves adorning the trees on both sides of the road, I wanted to switch off the air-conditioning and smell the fresh air but resisted the thought for the moment.

"Tell me about your family and work, Shekhar. Can I call you Shekhar?" I asked.

His eyes gleamed as he nodded. "At the age of 19, my Dad started his business with a small highway-side eating joint and later added a motel at the outskirts of Meerut* city. Not well-educated, he later made a big decision of moving to New Delhi where he set up his first serviced apartment hotel. Mom ran the kitchen and people came for the wonderful hospitality and amazing food. He stuck to his values and never allowed anti-social intrusions. He was always a family man in love with his wife.

"Real estate was booming, and so was the Indian economy. He started setting up more properties and attracted expat professionals and families for long-term stays. 'Central Kitchen' was simultaneously established and then he made his next big move to the US. He was the sole breadwinner of the family and went through some really tough times in the initial years of his business, something that Mother never allows us to forget."

PS leaned back in the car a bit. "The changing times were also conducive to the expansion of his business that grew manifold, with a range of highway motels along the National Highways across India as well as the US. In no time, he became the industry leader in the highway hospitality market – a niche market. After a few years, another transition happened, but I will leave that story for Dad to tell you; he has an interesting way of narrating it," he said, with a fond smile.

"Mom and Dad had an early marriage but the four of us were born at inconsistent intervals. Mom calls it God's will, whatever that means. My elder brother Kshitij is the one at the helm of affairs in the business currently as Dad is slowly phasing out of managing the daily business. Now, Kshitij Bhaiya* is at the top of things, like his name, or...at least I hope he is," he said, chuckling.

I could hear the fondness for his brother in his voice as he continued. "Actually, this car is also his...rather, it's one of his cars. He was too embarrassed to let me drive you in my tiny red Beetle and ordered me to pick you up in this car to give you a better view."

I nodded, acknowledging the efforts taken to make me feel at home. "I would like to breathe in the fresh air of the country side," I said, for I couldn't contain this desire anymore.

It also gave a small pause to the conversation as the cold, noisy wind embraced us when PS opened the rooftop of the car. I allowed the unpolluted countryside air to flow through my hair.

"Who else is there in the family?" I asked after sometime, once the familiar hum of the car air-conditioning returned.

"Kshitij Bhaiya went to London to pursue Business Administration and met Sugandha* there. She was a top ranker, mind you, and Bhaiya would only go for the best. They have a 17 year-old-son who I absolutely adore but Kshrey could do with some attention from his parents."

PS was in a flow and the tone was a bit caustic. I made a quick mental note of his remarks.

"And?" I probed further.

"Oh, there is my middle brother Dhruv and his wife, their two sweet kids, my wife, and yes, also my kid sister, who makes guest appearances at the house. Ours is an Indian joint family that has been given no option but to live together, under the same roof in the upmarket Lennox Hill area in the heart of New York City that we lovingly call Punj Home."

He laughed out loud and turned the car onto a wider street. The skyline, filling up with steel and glass structures, announced the departure of the calm and serene countryside that faded into non-existence. Our car was swarming along with a horde of other cars in the ever-busy city traffic. We had entered the city of New York and I had already begun to miss the freshness of the countryside.

PS halted the car in the porch of a huge, shining glass and steel building in Midtown Manhattan. "Welcome to the headquarters of the Punj Empire, Sir! We have arrived at our destination," PS announced.

"We have arrived, have we?" I looked at him and smiled gratefully.

> *A small narrative on a family speaks volumes of their desires, evolution, pains, and relationships. Shekhar had shared a lot, and now was the rest of the family's turn to do so. Yet, I suspected there was a very important role I was about to play in what promised to be a slowly unfolding drama.*

**5**

# LOOKING BACK - THE FATHER

The fifty-five-storied, shining glass and steel building seemed like an architect's utilitarian dream, with "The Punj" brightly etched on the front glass door.

The Spanish doorman opened the door politely for us and smiled at PS using just his eyes. In return, PS placed a hand on his shoulder and smiled back.

"Hi John, what's up, man?"

John shrugged his shoulder and flashed a smile that assured his boss that he was fine.

It was half-past-one as we entered the white-marbled, high-ceilinged lobby of the hotel-cum-office complex and I could feel the hunger pangs knocking at my stomach.

"I am hungry," I said, hoping that PS would arrange for some food to be brought.

He smiled, as though in anticipation of my hunger, and said, "Dad is waiting for us at the 55th floor lounge." He signalled to the Spanish doorman to take us to the top floor with a small halt on the 53rd. Doorman John turned in the owners' key in the private elevators for a non-stop journey to the 53rd floor.

The door opened on 53rd and a suave man with salt and pepper hair, wearing a pristine white business coat, entered the elevator. "Move," he signalled to John and turned towards me. I could see John's fist tighten and his torso stiffen as he turned in the key again.

"Hello, it is a pleasure to meet you finally, SK," the white ensemble addressed me. He put his hand out, "I am Kshitij Punj. Managing Director at Punj Empire."

PS smiled, but his smile was met by his elder brother's cursory nod. "Thanks PS, for informing me of your arrival," he said, pointing at the message he had received on his phone.

As I shook Kshitij's hand, I sensed how firm his handshake was, and thought it was an art he must have mastered with immense practice. Within a few seconds, we had reached the private lounge on the apex floor. A portion of the floor, it seemed, had been kept private.

John released the key and stared at Kshitij's back with fixed eyes as we moved out of the elevator.

We were ushered to an enormous private dining cabin by a discreet hostess. "SK Sir, so glad to finally see you! All that my old friend Yuri does is talk about you, every time he calls me or visits us. Show me your magic wand before we proceed any further," Prem* Prakash* Punj said, lifting his grand frame up from his plush sofa. He stepped forward to engulf me in an eager embrace, an old tradition followed by North Indians to welcome their visitors into their lives.

He said, "We have so much to talk about. I do not know where to begin!"

"Dad," Kshitij cleared his throat, "SK Sir must be hungry." He gestured subtly, asking his father to release me from his embrace. Grateful at that reminder, I picked up a plate and moved towards the food counter, led by PS. Senior Mr Punj and Kshitij sat around the large dining table to get their food served by the catering staff. There was a grand buffet spread but I am a man of limited needs. A ladleful of rice, lentil, and curd would do wonders for me that afternoon. I took my filling and returned to the table.

Senior Mr Punj was a reservoir of interesting tales. Seven decades of life including five decades of working had made him a stellar storyteller. "My journey started from a small 10x10 ft. shack on the roads to the dusty town of Meerut in India and ended at the headquarters in New York after thirty years. It was a bumpy road but a well-travelled one. God has been very kind. From owning a dhaba and a small motel in sleepy town of Meerut to headquarters in Manhattan in New York city, a city that never sleeps, it has been indeed an illustrious yet humbling journey for the Punj Empire," he said, with moist eyes.

Kshitij interjected at this point. "It was I who brought in the idea of expanding into the international markets. 57 motels across India are running successfully with minimum intervention from our end. We have a franchisee network of over 142 motels and hotels across US, 4 food-processing units within US, 3 fully owned lovely boutique hotels and 226 hotels being run by us in the world. Now,

I want to expand the business into the South American territory with hospitals and nursing units with the best in luxury, tapping into the large middle-class, while using technology. The low hanging fruits are cheap labour costs and ample opportunities for acquisition of smaller players. In fact, my best team of lawyers is, at the moment, working on a merger and acquisition on the floor below while we relish our caviar." He pointed at his plate as he said this, while I savoured my carrot and beetroot salad.

*My thoughts drifted towards the cherry trees by the lake at Central Park. I wondered if I would be fortunate enough to witness the Sakura (cherry blossom) bloom on the white cherry trees in New York as I had witnessed it the year before in Kyoto.*

Senior Mr Punj looked at his son with mixed sentiments, took a long pause at the sight of my drifting eyes and was about to speak, before Kshitij cut his father short. "Like any business, we also had our shares of bumps. Some big bumps too."

He nodded at me courteously as he began to make his way out, "If I can be excused, gentlemen, our new batch of Hotel Management graduates from Cornell are joining us this afternoon. We have recruited the best of the lot. I need to brief the team now. See you at home for dinner, SK. It will be our pleasure to host you in New York. Looking forward to spending some quality time with you."

He kissed his father on his forehead and whispered, "Easy, Dad, easy," and swiftly walked towards the elevator.

Senior Mr Punj regaled me with interesting stories from his past, his numerous associate-cum-friends across India, their business-specific peculiarities and the management issues every expanding business faces.

"I retired from active work earlier this year though I still come here as the Chairman of the Employee Welfare Board, a mute spectator who can watch things happening but not speak. Who does not like profit, SK Ji*? But it isn't always about numbers. The business needs to have some vision or value system. Who are we if not for our values?" The patriarch's words reflected his confusion and despondence. Senior Mr Punj let out a deep sigh and looked me in the eye as PS stepped away to take a call.

The Punj Empire was expanding and the expansion had come with a certain set of challenges, at work and at home. Senior Mr Punj wanted to discuss them in detail with me during my stay at their house. It was apparent now that it wasn't going to be easy, and I was yet to meet the other members of the Punj household.

PS was back and had a big smile on his face. "That was Simona on the phone, Dad. Our new Indian Diet Snacks' launch video has gone viral on the web in the US. People are going crazy over the Indo-Samba dance. Let me go and tell Kshitij and Dhruv Bhaiya," he said, unable to contain his excitement.

His habit of calling his elder brother respectfully by the Indian suffix of 'Bhaiya' was a habit that had survived time. He rushed towards the staircase. "See you later, Dad...Sir." He looked back and grinned before vanishing down the stairs.

"He is my mad boy," Senior Mr Punj said, with a grin that contained pride and worry about his son's wellbeing.

"You have to hear all the crazy stunts he pulls. Sometimes I wonder how he manages to handle marketing so well like a wizard, despite his absence from work for days at a stretch. I am not even half aware of what all he does in life! Now, since he is married, I am hoping that at least his wife can put a leash on him and make him more stable."

"Your other son, Dhruv, does he work from the same office?" I enquired.

"Yes, yes. Dhruv is based out of the 51st floor with his food production team. He likes to stay a bit mysterious and secretive. PS on 52nd and Kshitij on 53rd. Dhruv manages all functions of the food production units and often travels across the states for sales and operational matters. He should be somewhere on his floor, stuck in some crisis or other. If there are energies that attract crisis to a man, Dhruv is full of them. My poor child." Senior Mr Punj's worries were written all over his forehead in the form of the wrinkles that ran from side to side.

"And your daughter? Is she involved in the business too?" There was no mention of the women of the house in our conversation until I brought it up.

"Mynah! She is a free bird, true to her name. She is beyond business or other realms of real life. I spent all my life in managing business and did not realise how fast the kids had grown up. When Mynah, my last born, also grew up and flew away from the house, though a bit late, I realised it was time to give them a common bond and keep them together in the business and at home. Mynah is the only one who flew away from our nest but she keeps coming back to refuel her expenditure budget. I am trying to get her home while you are with us." He said this in a hushed tone for some strange reason.

"I would like to see your beautiful hotel and office floors," I said, veering the conversation away from what seemed to be an agonising note.

"Of course, SK Ji. It is my pride to show you around our hotel." Senior Mr Punj slowly moved towards the elevator, which was promptly opened by John, using his ready owner key.

He patiently took us to each floor, starting with the 54th, which housed predominantly grey conference rooms for Executive level meetings. The floor was abuzz with men and women in formal attire buried in their laptops or engaged in serious conversations. There were almost an equal number of men and women, making the Punj's an equal opportunity employer. Our next stop was the 53rd Floor. I couldn't help but breathe in a strong whiff of white lily on that floor. The entrance lobby was of white marble with the reception sparkling in white granite.

The offices had bare glass windows from ceiling to floor, and white leather furniture. On each table was a crystal vase with a large bunch of white lilies with one red rose in the centre, breaking the monotony of white in the environment. Then, I saw Kshitij giving a young, scared girl a serious run-down across the tall black leather table in his expansive office.

Senior Mr Punj told me in a hushed voice, "That poor girl is his Executive Assistant."

The girl was in tears but was not retaliating, nodding to accept the mistake she may not have even committed. I looked at Senior Mr Punj to move to a place where I could find some solitude. This was my own way of making notes.

Half an hour of solitude in a closed meeting room with glass windows gave me enough clarity to move ahead. Led by John, who was waiting for me, I came out and smiled at Senior Mr Punj, who was softly snoring in a comfortable lounge chair.

We went from floor to floor. The hotel was spread across 50 floors including the expansive lobby on the ground floor. Many wings were under renovation on Kshitij's command.

On the 52nd floor, Shekhar was in a huddle with his marketing team. As he handled global marketing for Punj Empire from the head office, the evening huddle was for a de-briefing on the US markets and plans for the Asian and European markets for the following day. India markets were to be discussed the next morning for a new digital media campaign for the Indian Diet Snacks launch.

"He is very excited about new hospitality trends emerging in India and wants to work extensively on new plans," Senior Mr Punj informed me.

The layout of the floor was basic, understated, and minimalistic. The floor looked much more spacious and alive than the other floors. PS waved at us, still beaming with his victory from the afternoon. As we moved towards the elevator, he came rushing towards us.

"I am taking the team out to celebrate and also witness my new musical performance at India Club. See you at home, Sir… Dad."

As we reached the 51st floor, I noticed eyebrows being raised. People looked suspiciously at me.

"Unfamiliar faces are not easily accepted on this floor," whispered Senior Mr Punj. "Operation and Sales teams of the food production department usually work within certain parameters and with limited people. They rarely get the opportunity to interact with others. Their journey starts on the ground floor and ends on this floor."

As I entered the elevator with Senior Mr Punj again, John bowed his head and addressed us with a "Señor" for the 24th time that afternoon.

As we descended in the elevator, visiting some floors and skipping others, I could feel a range of emotions flowing through me. Each floor looked like a silo in itself. The work environment was different, the people felt different. The only thing that remained constant was the people's respect and awe for Senior Mr Punj wherever we went.

Human Resources and Administration were in the basement with other supporting functions. A hotel is a maze where one is likely to get lost and not be found again. We decided to cover the rest of the hotel the next day.

For his age, Senior Mr Punj was very active. I wondered why he chose to retire instead of continuing to let his company benefit from his wisdom and expertise acquired over the years.

The sun was setting somewhere in the far West and the last rays of sunlight were falling on "The Punj" engraved in fading brass, as it offered its daily parting homage to the grand old man who had spent his blood and sweat to make the sun rise above this empire.

There was earnestness in Senior Punj. He had planned well, executed well, and reaped some great results, yet why was he restless? Why was I witnessing the strong tinge of uncertainty under his calm demeanour? Whatever caused this situation had to be examined through the symptoms to determine the cause. I needed to be alert. It was surely going to be more challenging than I had earlier assessed.

**6**

# 'WHY EXIST?' — THE YOUNGEST SON

The elderly Indian chauffeur smoothly drove Senior Mr Punj's BMW into the driveway of The Punj House. An elegant building in the splendour of Italian architecture with a private driveway, bougainvillea shrubs, lemongrass bushes, and perfectly trimmed low hedges greeted me. As we entered, I could see the street with its tall cedar, maple and pear trees and well-manicured lawns accentuate the beauty of the palatial house.

The house was fit to be the mansion of a king but thankfully, everyone in the house referred to it as a home to the Punj family and not a palace.

An elderly Indian butler opened the main door to let us into a large, four-storied, spacious and immaculately furnished house. He served us warm water in crystal glasses upon our arrival. He already knew of my preferences. As we settled into the living room overlooking the greens through large glass windows, a trail of aromatic mixed spices floated in the air, tantalizing my senses and alerting my stomach.

"Is it dinner time already?" I asked, for my watch read

1800hrs as per the Eastern Time Zone.

"The aroma you are relishing is of the savouries being cooked by my wife in your honour. Wait for her army of snacks to march in from the kitchen with a bevy of accompaniments. People used to die for them back in Meerut and New Delhi." Senior Punj chuckled softly, while leaning on his mammoth-sized chair's robust arm and twirling his thick white moustache.

"Oh! Hello, SK!"

I looked up, and my eyes met the intense eyes of an elegant, petite woman with shoulder-length salt and pepper hair.

I rose to greet her with folded hands. She wiped her wet hands on the sides of her white linen trousers and adjusted her long silk tunic to settle comfortably into a chair opposite me and greeted me with a Namaste* and a slightly bowed head.

Senior Punj said, "May I present my beautiful wife, Ana, our dear Annapurna* to you?"

"Annapurna. Your name is synonymous with the sumptuous food in front of us. But you shouldn't have been so formal in serving such an elaborate menu. I'm sure you are aware of my small appetite," I chided her gently.

She smiled again and said, "It is indeed my pleasure to take good care of our guests. By the way, I hope you liked the lunch."

"Our lunch is cooked at home and sent to the hotel everyday by Ana," Senior Punj explained.

"Do you cook all the food for the complete family yourself every day?" I asked with astonishment.

"Yes, each meal is cooked under my direct supervision. The kitchen is my war room just like hotels were his during all these years," she stated proudly.

"I agree. We all choose our own battlefields," I concluded, marvelling at her disclosure.

I absorbed the unfailing olfactory trail of lavender air freshener that followed me wherever I moved in the living room and lounge area. Looking around, I saw hues of violet throughout the living room. From the lavender curtains to the violet cushions and deep purple carpet, the house was a veritable valley of purple.

"Purple is the colour of prosperity. Ana is highly influenced by Feng Shui*," Senior Mr Punj answered my query.

The house smelled purple but had an aura of deep orange. I wondered why there was no whiff of aromatic flowers from the trees that greeted us in the driveway. Spring seemed to be blooming only outside The Punj Home.

"Ana likes to keep her house spic and span, she has no tolerance for untidiness. Not that New York is a dusty city but she is highly paranoid about cleanliness. So, all the windows and doors in this house are seal-proof. The whole house is air-conditioned. Did you notice the double door entrance of the house?" Senior Punj asked me, and I nodded.

It was apparent that Ana didn't like the city. As if confirming my thoughts, Sr. Punj stated, "What she would really like is to live in our country house in San Antonio, Texas. We fly there in our plane so very often. Just the two of us, spending time together like old times."

He was clearly lost in his memories and his love for Ana was unshakeably clear. How many couples had I come across who still loved each other after nearly 45 years of marriage?

As we were finishing our snacks, a beaming PS walked in. His energy was infectious and the room lit up upon his arrival.

Looking at me, he smiled and said, "I had a wonderful time, Sir! Are you up for a walk? I would like to share some thoughts with you," he said, pointing towards the door.

"Wait! Have some snacks before you go, PS," Ana promptly said, making her way to the kitchen.

Senior Punj excused himself to go freshen up and asked me if I wanted to settle in my room before dinner. I decided to step out for a walk with PS first.

*

The weather was bracingly cold. Spring had set in completely and I said a small prayer quietly to show my gratitude to Mother Nature for the bounty of beauty spread in our surroundings.

PS said, "Did you notice, Mom and Dad not even once asked me what was I excited about?" I could hear his silent sobs as he walked towards the garden with me. "I do not need food for stomach, I need warmth for my soul."

I looked at his sad eyes and held his hand. The emotional pain was flowing through his veins. "Tell me about your evening, Shekhar. Would you like to share?" I asked.

He narrated the events of the entire evening in a single breath. The Indian musical he was part of was planning a 15-day South Asian tour and they wanted Shekhar to accompany them. Shekhar was in two minds earlier due to work commitments and the promise made to his wife for a normal quiet weekend getaway the week after, though now she seemed all excited to spend some time in India during the tour.

"What is it that you want from life, Shekhar? What is it that you have in you to give to the society and the world?" I asked.

"I want to go to the extremes of life. I want to explore every part of India, the places, culture, cuisine, and lifestyle. I want to pursue music, theatre, drama, mountaineering, write travelogues, justify my role in the family business, be a good son, and an ideal husband... Phew!

"The expectations are immense from each role! My friends, family, spouse, team...everyone wants a slice of me and I have an eternal struggle that chases me all the time. I cannot decipher the meaning of existence. Why exist?" He sounded exasperated.

Before I could respond, he spoke again. "Why am I opening up to you with my deepest desires and secrets since the time we met? I have been to some shrinks before. They make you speak, make you cry, and at the end of the day, no results. Just a few justifications, and a feel-good factor for others around you."

He paused and spoke again, "I don't even know you, but I have heard you are different. Are you another shrink?"

There was a lingering pause between us. We were standing in front of a tall tree that had Shekhar's name on a placard nailed on to it. I looked at him. He smiled this time.

"I planted this willow oak when we moved into this house. Thus, my name on it."

I asked, "Have you ever asked this grown-up tree why it exists since you are the one who planted the seed? Do you own its future? Who decides what holds for him in future? An amazing intelligence is at work in this piece of creation and it knows how to exist. Do you mean you, a blessed human, full of intelligence, are finding it difficult to exist? Who is responsible for the growth of tree of your life?"

Shekhar looked at me completely lost for words after I probed him. Observant people are deep. He had only heard of it till now but had an opportunity to witness it today.

"Tell me Sir, are you really a mystic from Himalayas as Yuri Uncle had told me? He said that every life you touch turns into gold. You are an alchemist!" He held my hand again.

I laughed at his question and folded my hands.

*Some questions need to ripen well before answers grow on them.*

# 7

# TOO BUSY— DAUGHTER-IN-LAW & ELDEST SON

Shekhar walked me up to my designated room on the guest area of the 1st floor. He had promised to take his wife out for the latest Hindi* movie released in the city and planned to sneak out quietly with her lest his mother notice his absence from the dining table and create a case study out of it. We decided upon connecting again the morning after and he disappeared into the elevator to go to his room on the top floor of the house.

I settled into the room and called for the butler to help me open the soundproof window with an alley key. The butler, Sharat Ram*, was at first reluctant but then complied. I took a deep whiff of the orange aroma floating in the air, soaked in the pleasant noises from the garden and nearby central park, and welcomed colour in the pristine white guest room.

Soon, dinner was announced on a public announcement system that echoed across the house. The much-required tranquillity had helped me re-energise my senses and I was ready to meet the rest of the Punj family.

The elevator door opened and I saw two chirpy kids with a pleasant-looking young woman.

"Hi there!" I greeted her, smiling broadly. Kids have a natural way of engaging with the best of me. I bent down to shake their hands. They giggled again. We had reached the dining area where the elevator opened on the ground floor.

"Ah! I see you have met Sonam and her chipmunks!"

Senior Punj was waiting for us in the lobby.

"Yes, I am glad we met but we are yet to know each other," I said.

"Hi. I am Dhruv's wife, Sonam Punj. This is Sasha and that is Theertha," said Sonam, introducing herself and her six-year-old twins.

"Sonam is a champion soccer mom, SK. Her life revolves around school and activities; activities and school. You should look at these chipmunks making her run around the garden in the evening," said Senior Punj, his face beaming.

"Ah, yes, I heard them earlier in the evening today but could only place the laughter with the faces now."

I decided to sit between Sasha and Theertha on the table.

"Is Dhruv home yet? He was not there in office too," Senior Punj asked Sonam.

"No, Daddy. He will be back tomorrow. Some issue at the Chicago City manufacturing unit," Sonam responded.

"Any idea what it is about?" he enquired again.

Sonam seemed to be at a loss for words. I could see the helplessness floating in her eyes.

> *A spouse is a pillar of strength at home; someone with an independent vision, goal, and purpose in life, but in sync with you more than anyone else in the world. Men or women who are deprived of this insight do not know what they are missing out on in life.*

As the dinner was being served, Sasha and Theertha regaled me with stories from their school, summer camp, swimming classes, and piano lessons. They talked of their aspirations to learn skiing and archery when they turned eight.

Sonam's life revolved around living the kids' present and planning their future. She was living her twin daughters' lives. She had their life all planned out as she wanted to ensure that they did not miss out on anything like she had. She talked of her experience with the other mothers at school and got nostalgic about her carefree college days in New Delhi before moving to the US to be with her husband's family.

The elaborate dinner served in front of us was enough to feed a small army. There were just few of us on the dining table. Ana joined the table after dinner was served. I could see that she had not taken the absence of Shekhar and his wife (and of Kshitij and his wife too) at the dining table kindly, but the Punjs' believed in keeping their displeasure private.

By the end of the dinner, through Ana, I knew of every ingredient and condiment that went into each dish on the table.

Sonam excused herself from the dining table to put her kids to bed. Ana went back to the kitchen to get us some coffee. The loud honking of a car was heard in the driveway and the double entrance doors opened abruptly. After a few moments, in walked Kshitij Punj and a middle-aged woman in an immaculate three-piece business suit. I recognized her to be the lady we came across on the M&A floor in the office building. They were in the midst of a heated argument as they entered the room but went quiet at the sight of Senior Mr Punj and me in the living room.

Kshitij said, "Oh! Hi, SK. I almost forgot you would be home with us tonight. My apologies, I missed out on the dinner with you. That must have left Mum really angry."

The woman in the three-piece business suit collected her nerves and extended her hand. "Hi, I am Sugandha, Senior Partner at Punj Empire and better half of Kshitij Punj." She looked at Kshitij and smiled but was still visibly distracted. Ana was out of the kitchen with a frown on her face directed at her elder son and daughter-in-law at the table.

"How did the day go, Kshitij?" Senior Punj asked gently. "I witnessed some disruption on your floor earlier today."

"Oh, you saw that. It was nothing, Dad. Sara changed the whole chronology of the presentation for the new Cornell Grads joining today. I mean, who kept her there to use her brains? She should follow the instructions to the tee. This week has been very hectic and I can't afford to have any more disruptions." Kshitij ranted with his mouth full of food, putting aside the immaculate culinary etiquettes he had displayed during lunch. "Hmm. By the way, what is the colour of peace, Sugandha?" he asked his wife.

"Blue or green," Sugandha responded. Senior Punj had mentioned at the hotel that she had a keen eye for aesthetics and décor.

"Perfect," Kshitij said, snapping his fingers and calling his butler. "Ram, please send a bunch of Petunias, err no, blue Orchids with a bottle of the finest Castelvetrano Olives to Sara's residence tonight."

He looked at his wife and said, "I can't afford to have her miss the entire week ducking under an emotional trauma over today's incident. I may have over-reacted too, but who asked her to use her brain?"

He got back to his tuna salad. They finished their dinner quickly. Both Kshitij and Sugandha were light eaters. Sugandha excused herself from the table as she had to get back to her room to finish the M&A final documents.

Standing by the elevator, she turned and asked, "Oh, I forgot to ask. Mom, has Kshrey eaten already? I didn't see him around."

"Shekhar took Kshrey along with Neha and him to watch a Hindi movie, Sugandha. He seems more close to his uncle than the two of you together," Ana said. "Not that it absolves Shekhar of the crime of wasting my food today but I have to give him the credit for pseudo-parenting your son while giving him some good values too."

Sugandha turned deaf ears to her mother-in-law's sarcasm and entered the elevator, waving to the rest of the people in the living room.

Kshitij walked up to me and said cheerfully, "Give me 15 minutes, SK. I will take you to witness a life that you cannot even fathom. I mean, it has been a long week and I need to hit the gym at 6am, but what the heck? See you in a bit." He rushed up the stairs to go to his room on the 3rd floor to freshen up and change.

"Mighty energetic boy my elder one is," Senior Mr Punj said, looking at a spot in the distance. "Who would say he has crossed four decades of existence with that lean build? Unlike his father, he has learnt to balance his life. Well almost, most of the time only when he is not in a rush, which is forever."

He then turned towards me.  "It took me twenty years to build my hotel and food business in India. I grew slowly and steadily, working 18 hours a day. I do not recollect ever taking a Sunday off. Maybe a Holi* or Diwali*, or an odd family holiday to the children's maternal grandmother's house."

He continued, "My life was all about work. After we moved to the US, Kshitij studied in London, which was his dream, married and got Sugandha along upon his return home. Twenty years in the US and look at how our businesses have expanded. You heard about their plan to expand by acquiring hospitals in South America. Kshitij is raising huge loans, hiring the best of talent, working long hours but everything seems disjointed. We are spread thin all over. SK, I am fearful that once I am gone, all that I built brick-by-brick will shatter into pieces. My family and business...both would disintegrate. I know what I have created in my children."

He had tears in his eyes by then, as he recounted the happy and painful moments in his life. "I started my business with a vision to establish a quality hospitality brand with Indian pride intact, but with these expansions and mergers, I am not sure where we are headed. Kshitij is too ambitious and is running a race that has no finish line. Unfortunately, I know where it ends. And he won't listen. He is growing into the demon Ravana*, super-intelligent but lustful."

He turned towards the mammoth dining table with its hardly consumed food on the top. "Despite our personal differences, Ana and I insisted that no matter what happens, our family would live under the same roof and work under the same company. And here we are. Living together, eating on the same dining table but everyone retreats back to their own silos. There is no connect, no engagement with one another. They don't even fight with each other any longer." He cupped his chin with his hands in despair and terminated his train of thought.

I patted him gently on his back, saying a silent prayer.

"Can you help us, SK, in saving ourselves from destroying our own selves?" He looked at me with tearful eyes and turned away as soon as he heard Kshitij rushing down the stairs.

Kshitij proclaimed, "Ok, I am raring to enhance the experiences of your life, SK!" He flashed a big smile and asked me, "How willing are you?"

I smiled back and said, "A 100%!"

# 8

# LIFE IS A JOURNEY— THE DAUGHTER

The black Porsche Cayman glided down the smooth New York roads. The air was breezy and I enjoyed the sight of the illuminated tall buildings and the buzz in the city that never sleeps.

"Only a sporty car can do justice to a man with a sportsman's physique. It is a tough job to be in the top league in everything you do in life and still be adored by everyone alike." Kshitij glided his hand on the leather back of my seat and showered himself in words filled with self-praise.

I smiled at his dual pride but said nothing.

He continued his monologue. "It is a big week ahead for me. I am putting everything that I have at stake for the new business acquisition.

"There were traitors I had kept for a long time but I finally got rid of them last month. It had been really tough on the company to sack some of our top people but change is an inevitable, although painful process. Unlike in India, an

American employee's retrenchment is a tricky business but I managed well, I guess."

He continued, "Although there is nothing that I cannot handle in life, I am convinced that trust is the most mistrusted word in the corporate world and difficult to command."

I was curious at his excessive use of "I" in the expression for a family business with many stakeholders but nodded to acknowledge that I was hearing him out.

I asked,  "Where are we headed, Kshitij?"

"Provocateur, SK. I would have rather taken you to 1 OAK, but most of the crowd seems to be avoiding 1 OAK tonight. Perhaps another time," he responded. "It is a heaven-on-earth for party lovers. Do you enjoy letting down your hair sometimes, SK?" he asked.

I ran my left hand through my ponytail and laughed out loud.

The valet took the car away with utmost courtesy and we confronted the long queues that formed outside the swanky nightclub in the basement of an upmarket hotel in the Meatpacking district.

Entry to the club was not an issue for Kshitij. The nods and intimate 'ayes' he received from glittery women on our way into the bar was an indication that he was no stranger to the place and the people here.

"Please feel free to order a drink of your choice, SK. I just spotted my golfing gang across the club, will say a quick hello and return." He patted my shoulder and disappeared into the crowd across the room.

I ordered my drink and stood by the ledge, gazing across at the LED illuminated staircases. The giant Egyptian phoenix wings suspended from the ceiling grabbed my attention. I had seen their latest club that opened in the Four Seasons Dubai, but this one was the original! I found myself tapping my feet and humming to the music being played by Nick M.

Kshitij was back in no time, saying, "This is a private party and I am on every private party's invitation list. I am ordering my drink. Can I get you a refill of what you are having?" he asked.

I nodded. The waiter arrived.

"One Jim Beam Black, large for me." He turned towards me after ordering and whispered, "Nothing but the best for me."

I asked the waiter for another Vanilla Milkshake. "More ice, no sugar."

Kshitij gaped at me and asked, "Vanilla Milkshake. Is that what you were grooving on?"

I laughed and rested my hand on his shoulder. "I live in a permanent state of intoxication, Kshitij. The source is within."

The club was getting crowded by the minute. I could spot many celebrities under the blinding lights and smoke-filled rooms. There was intrigue and ecstasy filled furore in the club. Eventually, the crowd began settling down in familiar corners with the shift in the mood of the music. The DJ was playing psychedelic trance.

I noticed a young, spirited Indian woman bending down on the music console and directing the DJ to slow the music down further. She wore a long, flowing white robe with a shining golden belt, and crystal beads around her slender neck. Her shoulder-length hair flowed till her hips and her lips were moving, as though she was praying silently. Many amongst the crowd that had walked in earlier were dressed similarly, in long flowing white gowns but with silver belts. If it weren't for her attire, I would have taken her for someone who had been to the other side of sanity and back.

She opened her eyes and walked towards us. "Namaste, Kshitij Bhaiya." She folded her hands and bowed. Her hands folded away from her body at the neck level.

"Mynah, we were expecting you home today. You knew we had an important guest from India with us." He glared at her as he shouted to be heard.

"Stop shouting, Bhaiya. I can hear you," she reacted sharply. "You know I am on a different tangent of life and have taken a responsibility to help all these people, help them enlighten their lives with the ultimate truth. Why do you bother to even ask me to come home knowing how busy I am?" She shot back at him in a flat voice, barely audible, while pointing at all the people in white robes.

Kshitij turned towards me and did a quick introduction to his sister to prevent anyone overhearing any further exchange of heated words. "SK, this is my baby sister, the enlightened one, Mynah Punj."

I folded my hands and bowed at the spirited girl.

"Namaste. Are you a mystic?" she asked.

I laughed and retorted, "Are you?"

She nodded her head and began philosophising. "Life is a journey. I have attained peace, experienced nirvana. Do you see all these people there? They call me their Master. I feel responsible for cleansing their souls. How can Mum or Dad expect me to be home when I have taken such a big burden on my shoulders? I know that it is a long and lonely journey. Not even my shadow will walk with me to the end of this journey but I need to be tough in order to achieve the purpose of my life. Meditate more, experience my soul deeply, and help all these people connect with their souls."

I was bemused with her ability to carry on prolonged monologues without any eye contact or acknowledgement from the listener.

"But you have so much to gain from practical life. You are barely a day older than 25," Kshitij retorted.

She kept quiet, looking away.

"Are you drunk, Mynah?" he demanded, enraged.

"I have seen it all since I was 13. I am drunk with spirituality tonight. I have been on the other side and back. Gone even beyond. Don't you know that?" she retorted and then took my hand into hers to lead me somewhere.

The sleeves of her gown fell away and I noticed purple veins and deep cuts on her forearm that narrated fading tales of the pitfalls of a youth gone astray.

She said, "Let me give you a 360-degree tour of the city from the terrace of this hotel, SK, and then we can head back home to Mum's kitchen with Bhaiya."

She signalled to her group and they bowed down to her and exited the club. We then headed upstairs. After our brief terrace tour near the pool, she showed me the west side highway that looked like a runway with tiny lights shimmering from a distance.

"Life is a highway or a runway. What an illusion. Such confusion." She looked at me and laughed out loud.

*

We returned together in the car, where Kshitij had gone completely quiet. Mynah chirped, "Dad mentioned about your influence on the business communities and intelligent people in India when we spoke last."

She seemed like a different person from the one I had met an hour ago, when she started talking about the changing economy and emerging HR trends in India. I learnt that she had completed her masters in human relations after graduating with double majors in philosophy and the history of religions before turning completely towards spirituality. She had also tried to pursue research but dropped it mid-way.

"I was actually looking forward to a deep discussion on meditation and renunciation from the world with you during your visit," she said, after a brief pause.

"Why renunciation from the world?" I asked her. "Ok, tell me Mynah, how do you do meditation? How does it benefit you?"

"Oh, we all sit together in an energy infused space. All the souls blessed by our Holy Mother create a positive aura around us by chanting mantra given by our Supreme Master and we experience the power of our Holy Mother. This takes us into the beautiful world of trance. The invigorating energy of sandalwood beads necklaces and incense sticks fills us with the beauty of the senses. In the darkness of the room, we experience the Divine Light of the Almighty injecting into our souls." She narrated the process as though in a trance.

We had reached the Punj home. As Kshitij parked the car, Mynah and I walked towards the double door entrance to the house.

"Does this bring you peace of mind?" I inquired, looking into her eyes.

She didn't respond, just looked at me. "It feels wonderful with the eyes closed, doesn't it?" she asked me, on a completely unrelated note. "So nice, that I don't feel like opening my eyes again," she said.

"Living with eyes open is an imperative need. That's the expression of our interiority. Tell me how you feel about life with eyes open?" I probed.

This time something came over her. She stopped walking and instead of entering the door, held me by my shoulder and spoke once again, "Who are you? Why am I feeling a surge of reality dripping into me? And you're correct! Despite following a robust spiritual process, when my eyes are closed, I get transported to a different world with peace and tranquillity but the moment I open my eyes! Oh yes, you are right! I feel lonely and dejected. I want to run away from my parents and the rest of the world. It is as if my alternative soul takes over my life and creates chaos all around. This duality does not let me be at peace with myself. Am I creating an illusion of justifications around me? Am I hallucinating?"

She had found the right questions.

"We could work on a solution for this together, Mynah," I reassured her, as Kshitij joined us.

I could see her in deep thought, a bit disoriented, walking away. I was hoping that she would not consume another chemical to douse the fire of these questions.

# 9

# WHAT IS LIFE? — THE GRANDSON

I could not sleep well after the previous night's conversation and woke up early to re-energise myself through my practices. After two hours, with a fresh mind and gratitude in my heart, I resolved to make the new day better for the world than the previous day. It is the first thought that one gives to the subconscious early in the morning that sets the tone of the day. A while ago, I acknowledged the fact that I am a mere speck of dust in the grand scheme of the universe.

It is through my daily minuscule contribution that I aim to repay the universe, even if it is a fraction of what the universe has blessed me with. Humility is a virtue, pride is a vice but the line between the two is very thin. Tread carefully, I told myself as I stepped out to enjoy the glory of the morning sun and decided to take a walk around the Central Park close to The Punj House.

Just as I prepared to leave the expansive private lawns to step out towards Central Park, I saw a tall young boy with a drawing pencil in hand, his freckled face buried into the large canvas in front of him.

I stood behind him, mesmerized, without uttering a single word lest I break his concentration. My eyes were witnessing a marvel of nature being replicated on the huge canvas.

He drew a mammoth tree surrounded by vines clinging on to the tree but not reaching up to even its upper trunk. He covered the large tree with a rainbow of smiling colours but the vines had been painted in various hues of grey.

He stood back and gazed at his creation. I clapped slowly. Startled, the young boy turned around. His face was ashen as if someone had caught him stealing something from Nature.

"Good Morning, I'm SK. You must be Kshrey," I said, extending my right hand and the shy boy moved toward to shake my hand with his left. A left-handed marvel, I could see.

I felt immensely proud of this young boy. I found an instant connection with. "My son, who is 18 now, is left-handed too," I told him. "They are blessed with certain strengths that the right-handed strive for. Will you walk with me? I'm headed towards the Central Park."

He nodded and immediately started off with me without pausing to inform anyone. He seemed keen to know more about my son. We talked about his school and family, my family, and painting as a hobby as we walked together.

"What were you drawing? It looked symbolic to me," I asked.

He looked into my eyes and said softly. "Hmm. The large tree is my grandfather."

He continued, "Sometimes, I do not understand what life is, it's so confusing. I seem to have everything money can buy. My family can afford to have the best luxuries money can afford, but I see almost everyone running after something that has no name. Is life a chase? Is there a light at the end of the tunnel? Why a constant search for thrill? I studied in science that physiological needs are at the bottom of the human needs pyramid but I see everyone around me running after them all the time. Will we ever rise above the basics? We seem so bound by our physical needs!"

He was agitated. I looked at him affectionately.

He said, "Are these complicated questions from a 17-year-old? All I want to do is paint, paint, and paint. Play music like Shekhar Uncle, or some days, drive a sports car like my Dad...but my wants vary. I run to extremes. Life seems to be going everywhere yet I am stationed at one spot."

He looked at me and asked again, "Tell me, SK, what is this all about?"

"Do you know the meaning of your name, Kshrey?" I asked him.

He shook his head and said, "No. I don't."

"Kshrey means marvellous. You are your name, Kshrey. Remember that for today and the rest would be worth your wait," I said, patting his back.

We indulged in some talk about college life and his aspirations. On finishing the walk, I headed towards my room.

*My head was full of questions that needed compartmentalizing and processing. The problems are universal. It is the journey of emulating interiority over exteriority is what people find tough to imbibe in their lives. Otherwise, solutions are universal too.*

A few hours of practices in the room and my mind was uncluttered again. Solutions would emerge. Clarity was the seed for innovation and my mind was now light and free. It was not yet the opportune time to talk about the possible solutions.

The public announcement system blared that breakfast for office-goers was being served. I walked down the stairs to the dining table. A middle-aged, short man with ruffled hair was seated in the chair at the head of the table. He looked up as I made acquaintance with him.

"Good Morning. I am SK," I said, extending my hand to the one family member I hadn't interacted with yet.

The man measured me up and said, "Hello, I am Dhruv. Dhruv Punj." He stammered a bit as he gingerly shook my hand.

I looked at Dhruv Punj. This man was conspicuous by his absence on the food production floor at office yesterday.

Those whispering employees, mistrust amongst team members, and the hostile environment on the floor spoke of the leadership traits of the man with ruffled hair in front of me who was shy to look me in the eye. He was quite a handsome man in his own way and his reluctance to communicate added some charm to his mysterious personality.

"All well at the snacks factory, Beta* Ji?" Senior Mr Punj asked, joining us on the other side of the dining table.

"Yes Daddy Ji. I took care of it all," Dhruv said, brushing aside Senior Mr Punj's query.

"Good morning, everyone!" A loud voice emerged, attracting everyone's attention. It was Sugandha, who joined the others at the breakfast table.

"Dhruv, we need unit number 4 to be ready for the new business line productions in a month. Hope you have the buy-in from your top sharks," Sugandha threw a barb at Dhruv.

"It is an utter transgression in my work area, Sugandha. Mail me the final T&C and we will talk."

And that's all I had from Dhruv that day, since he got up to leave.

Sugandha gave Dhruv a cold stare and quickly finished her fresh juice before rushing to the door to call her chauffeur.

I turned to look at Senior Mr Punj." Are Mrs Punj and Mynah joining us for breakfast?" I enquired.

"So, you met Mynah finally," Senior Mr Punj, said, with a pleasant smile.

I nodded affirmatively.

"No, Mynah and Mrs Punj have a two-hour-long religious ritual regime before they eat in the morning. Please do grace the table, SK Ji," he said, gesturing to me to join him.

I breathed in the strong whiff of freshly sprayed lavender air-freshener in the room and sipped my green smoothie.

*

The day was spent at the hotel and the office, meeting key team members, holding further interactions with family members and inspecting the floors under renovation at the hotel and listening to stories of twenty glorious years of growth under Senior Punj by their loyal staff, who looked upon him as their mentor and messiah.

I chanced upon the elderly doorman, John, outside the hotel on my way out, and my conversation with him revealed a lot. He was angry with his own sons for wasting his hard-earned money. He also compared them to the elder sons of Senior Mr Punj who, according to him, were about to bring down the empire created by their father.

The air at the hotel was thick not only with hostility amongst many people, but the atmosphere was also clogged due to the untapped potential and the unexplored possibilities of people.

*Whatever is created comes to an end and this is a certainty as long as there is no one to keep creating after we are gone. Punj House was making the noises of the end. Something needed to be done. Do the right thing to get the right result. It was now time to find that out.*

# 10

# CONTEMPLATION

I requested for dinner in my room and left instructions that I should not to be disturbed till the next morning. There was much that was brewing in my mind. Getting into an introspective mode, I reflected over the events and interactions over the previous three days and opened my diary where all my observations about each person were registered.

*A diary is a reflection of one's thoughts and actions, a journal for the mathematics of life recorded at the end of each living day. Journal writing was a habit I inculcated in my youth, nurtured as an adult, and my diary has become an invaluable companion of life.*

Thus, my readings about each family member's observations, questions, and traits, some clear and some needing clarification, were there on the pages in front of my eyes.

*

Kshitij: His name is the Hindi word for pinnacle. He was looking for his place and lived under the illusion of having all the capabilities and qualities to claim that spot. He assumed the top spot was his birthright. His blurred vision limited him from understanding micro-details critical to successful execution. He needed people to do his thinking as well as planning. Building relationships required an unbiased and non-judgmental approach towards others; quite an alien concept to Kshitij.

Dhruv: A Hindi word for the North Star. He was a rock. An introvert. Insecure, but a family man. Loyal. Needed unquestioned followership. Lacked the ability to engage with people.

Shekhar or PS: A Hindi word for the peak or the top. He was sensitive and contemplative. Willing to sacrifice for the common good. Had creativity along with leadership traits. Could apply concepts and learning. Had great abilities to engage with himself and people around him. Was adventurous but conservative.

Mynah: The name of a bird. She was full of life. Needed her space and freedom. Wanted to understand life and was highly engaging with people. Didn't hesitate to explore new ideas. Had a great understanding of emotions, their cause and effect.

Kshrey: a Hindi word meaning "worthy of credit". This grandson was looking for the deeper meanings of life. He was an explorer of another dimension where physical life lost significance. His insightful approach lacked experience, which was adequately compensated by his querying mind. He looked for answers where most didn't even see a question.

Senior Punj: An ambitious man who was clever and

engaging; a storyteller who remained loyal to his people. He knew how to care for those he called his own. He didn't hesitate in asking for help and respected those who offered it. His humility and affection made up his personality. He led and followed, both at the same time. He was a visionary who could see his goals as well as his obstacles.

The Punj family had internal conflicts, which were starting to become visible in other family members and their businesses as well. Business and life growth opportunities existed yet could be tapped only if each individual's inner and inter personal strife was settled.

The plans made by Kshitij for expansions had borne fruits in the past and the group had grown. Yet, the foundations were weakening. The intent behind this growth was contaminating the roots. The family itself was disintegrating.

Those who consider life is only about them, find engagement with others a challenge. Disengaged, their family suffers and leaves them, followed by them getting surrounded by professionals who work with the approach of mercenaries, out to prove something to the world. It becomes a gang of insecure, disengaged people whose only motto in life becomes self-fulfilment. Such people and organisations become a source of intense misery; sugar-coated in niceness, comforts and some great HR practices.

Punj was at the beginning of such an end!

With such strengths and observations of the key family members written down in my journal, I started analysing their desires, challenges, and the possible solutions in their lives. At this, I now closed my eyes and went into a region beyond cognition, beyond thought, beyond logic and...a new pattern emerged in my mind.

*There was a moment of epiphany.*

# 11

# DESIRES

To understand this new pattern, one needs to start from the beginning...and everything begins with Desires!

Some say, "Desires cause suffering." Such people believe that it is not possible to keep running after desires! Consequently, according to them, we must desire in moderation.  Such wise people suggest ways to rein in the desiring mind. How does one do that? Desires are unlimited and cause conflicts in life.

Conversely, others say, desires are the very fuel to human progress and evolution; that walking the roads of desires is the very aim of life!

Over the years of our growth, we experience desires in the physical, mental and emotional dimensions of our life. A number of these desires arise through a constant compulsive mechanism triggered and controlled sometimes by the hormones produced in our body or sometimes through our interaction with the competitive world.

Through such compulsions, we produce emotions like those of self-rejection, need for approval, need for acceptance, jealousy, envy, greed, the need to win at all times, doubt including self-doubt, lust for power, lust for sex, need for isolation, dislike, irritability, anger, need for fame, need for visibility, cowardice, impulsiveness, attention-deficit and obsessive behaviours, etc. Thereafter, our entire life becomes a struggle wherein all that we are trying to do is overcome these emotional compulsions, or the guilt that accompanies these compulsions.

Nowadays, with greater access to information, we have started living in the illusion of being knowledgeable! In reality, we are justifying our guilt and compulsiveness with loads of information-based knowledge. This is a serious situation that needs some serious resolution. Since this entire chain of emotions is caused by desires which are making us compulsive...what shall we do? And what shall we not do?

As a next step, we need to understand that desires in themselves do not cause suffering. Desires, when fulfilled, give pleasure. When they remain unfulfilled, they cause pain and grief. This means that the real solution lies in creating an understanding of our desires. If we can create this understanding, then we will actively engage in working towards the fulfilment of our desires and produce pleasure in place of unfulfilled desires, which in turn, produces pain and misery!

To create this understanding, we need to see how our desires are formed.

Humans are blessed with 5 senses. Without these functional senses of touch, hearing, sight, smell, and taste, our understanding and experience of this world would be absent. Look at a sleeping person. In this state of sleep, our senses go into a partial shutdown mode. Our experience of the world reduces and we travel within ourselves. Patients in a coma have functional body organs but their experience of the world is negligible simply because there is some complication in either the sensory receptions, pathways of sensory data to the brain or sensory data management system inside the brain. Thus we can conclude that we receive data through these senses and when our brain processes this data, an experience gets created. This experience is understood through thoughts.

This means that as we receive more of the data through the senses, it creates more thoughts. This also means that a healthy sensory system with a properly functional sensory transmitting system and a healthy brain will produce more thoughts. Thus, a human who has more thoughts has a healthy and working brain. Thought making is an automated process.

Desires are also nothing but thoughts produced by our brain. Desires are those thoughts that give us a signal of either a forecasted pleasure or forecasted pain.

If desires are mere thoughts being produced by our brain and the brain is an important organ in our body, then why do we wish to reduce or control our thoughts? Why should we desire less? We never wish for our heart to stop or reduce functioning. Just like the function of our heart is to pump blood very efficiently and non-stop, similarly the brain's function is to produce thoughts and create vivid images. Why would we wish our brain to work with low efficiency?

If we cannot control desiring, does this mean we are destined to suffer, since we cannot fulfil all that we desire?

In order to answer this question, we need to understand that as humans, we are blessed with intelligence. But having intelligence doesn't guarantee the use of intelligence. Those humans with an enhanced ability to use their intelligence accomplish greater success. It is a simple formula. The more we use our intelligence, the more our desires get fulfilled. This means that our ability to choose which desires to chase, backed up by a choice of when, with whom and how to chase them, is called using our intelligence. An intelligent person will know which desire to chase right now!

Having understood the concept of the formation of desires, we no longer wish to chase the idea of moderation or curtailment of desires. We are fine with more desires as long as we can choose which desire to chase and which to ignore. Our senses and the brain producing more thoughts no longer traumatise us, because we can choose among the many desires that we may have and our focused action will no longer require determination and will power. We will naturally and joyfully execute our plans since we have made clear choices! However, these choices are possible only when we can understand the structure of desires.

And how do we understand our desires? How do we prioritise them? How do we decide to choose some, chase some, delay some, wait for some, and drop some?

# 12

# THE SUCCESS QUADRANT

I picked up my journal and drew a large quadrant.

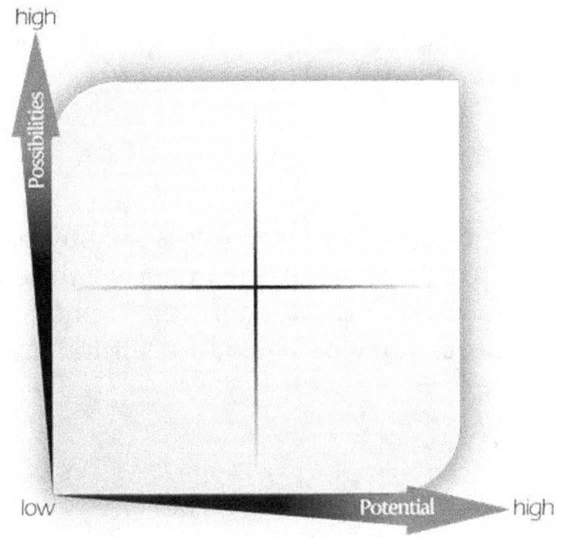


On the X Axis, I planted Potential.

On the Y Axis, I planted Possibility.

Experientially, I had known only two directions or dimensions in my life, one was the inside and the other was the outside. These were the only two existentially correct directions. The rest was relative. What is up when I am in the US is down in India. If two people point their finger in the upward direction at these two places at the same time, they are actually pointing towards opposite directions. Even North, East, West and South are existentially incorrect. They are in relation only to the planet and the planet is moving all the time. For a human being, his/her interiority and his/her exteriority are the only existentially correct directions, as my Master had said one day with an intoxicating laughter. They hold true for anyone, anywhere, anytime!

Based on these two directions emerged the concept of Possibility and Potential.


## POSSIBILITY

Our external world is a possibility. It is the physical world or situations over which we have none or little control. This again consists of other people, their emotions, their skill sets, trade, country policies, and cultural or national conflicts.


## POTENTIAL

My internal world is my potential. My potential is something that is completely under my control. Myself, or I, consist of 4 aspects: my body, my mind, my emotions and my energy.

I started writing in each quadrant:

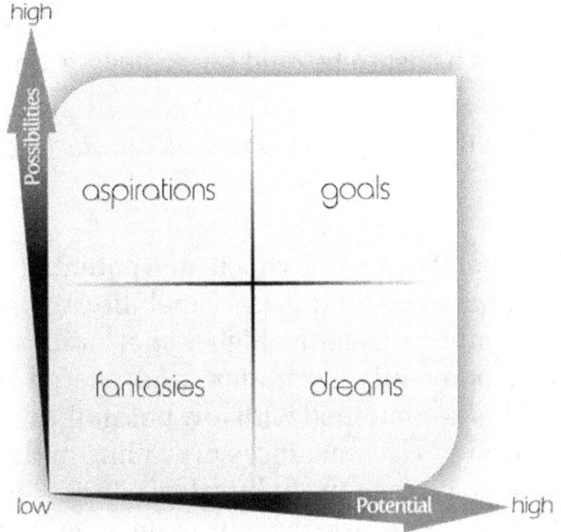



*Where **Potential** was <u>low</u> and **Possibility** was <u>low,</u> I wrote*
***FANTASIES.***

A Fantasy is that desire for which we possess low potential meaning low ability or capability, poor internal strength, low belief, poor skill, inappropriate attitude. In short, it is the poor alignment of our body, mind, emotion and energy. This is combined with a low possibility meaning a poor situation or circumstances prevailing in the world, country, industry, society, political scenario, economy, infrastructure, or other such external situations over which we have little to no control.

Those who chase fantasies accomplish little in their lives and end up with more failures. They live lives of ignorance. This usually results in low productivity for such people. Organisations that trigger more of fantasies or have more people living in the fantasy quadrant of desires, end up achieving less and talking more. Fulfilling a fantasy requires a dedication, which drops everything else in life. Even then it does not guarantee success. However, such people end up achieving something new and "out of the world". There is a cost to be paid for achieving fantasies.

*Where **Potential** was <u>High</u> and **Possibility** was <u>low</u>, I wrote* **DREAMS.**

A Dream is that desire for which my potential is high. This means I have the ability, the capability, the skill, the attitude, the inner strength, high belief, and a proper alignment of body, mind, emotion, and energy towards this desire. This is combined with low possibility, meaning a poor situation or circumstances prevailing in the world, country, industry, society, political scenario, economy, infrastructure or such external situations over which we have little to no control.

Those chasing only their dreams live quite a miserable life. This is so because their potential is high but situations do not permit them to accomplish their desires. For a human with high potential, failure due to external circumstances causes great misery. Initially such people invest their beliefs in various Gods and God men followed by disillusionment. They may slowly lose all their hope and suffer lives of distress and depression.

*Where **Potential** was <u>low</u> and **Possibility** was <u>high</u>, I wrote* **ASPIRATIONS.**

An Aspiration is that desire where we have a low potential meaning low ability or capability, poor internal strength, low belief, poor skill, inappropriate attitude, in short poor alignment of our body, mind, emotion and energy. This is combined with a high possibility meaning good or great situations or circumstances prevailing in the world, country, industry, society, political scenario, economy, infrastructure, or other such external situations over which we have little to no control.

Those chasing their Aspirations accomplish far more and their key to success is "internal change". These are those people who emerge as natural leaders and are constantly seeking greater evolution. Yet, people who chase only aspirations do not remain joyful. Their life remains a constant run. There are chances when they may easily fall off their path, though getting up and getting back is also easier for them. All in all, a much nicer space to be in!

*Where both **Potential** and **Possibility** were <u>high</u>, I wrote **GOALS.***

Goals are those desires for which my potential is high. This means I have the ability, the capability, the skill, the attitude, the inner strength, high belief and a proper alignment of body, mind, emotion and energy towards this desire. This is combined with a high possibility, meaning good or great situations or circumstances prevailing in the world, country, industry, society, political scenario, economy, infrastructure, or other such external situations over which we have little to no control.

Those who chase goals accomplish consistent and joyful success. Their lives are an example for others. They live in each moment and are the most productive people. They are the pride of the families they belong to and the organisations where they work.

Success is all about our ability to fulfil desires consistently. In order to fulfil desires, we need to understand what we desire. After this, we need to segregate these desires in a manner that we can intelligently choose which desire is to be chased. A foundation of failure is laid the moment we start chasing a desire that is not a goal.

*

I now wondered how this realisation would help me, or anyone else, become a consistent high achiever. And the answers came in rapidly.

Those who chase goals produce a great inner belief and confidence that will be based on the results they have had in their lives. Such people will no longer need any external motivation. Rather, they will be productive performers!

With this belief, they will invest in their self-development and learning, which will be specifically directed towards their aspirations. As they harness more of their Potential, their results produce belief and they earn the trust of everyone around them. They become the leaders naturally, since they know the path to success, for they know "how to fulfil desires".

This life state will lead them to invest hope in their dreams. They will have the necessary patience to wait out the tiding over of adversities. They will keep achieving their goals and aspirations while external situations either sort themselves out, or they collaborate with people who can help resolve external situations. This way, their dreams begin to be realised. Those who chase dreams alone, without following this success quadrant, end up losing faith and hope and become miserable. But those who are constantly achieving and are productive, they live with renewed vigour and energy and wait for the right time to realise their dreams!

It is for such people who have developed such internal balance and stability and who have an unending list of accomplishments in the form of their goals, aspirations, and dreams, who end up chasing their fantasies without losses in any area of their life! They are the true innovators who work not out of obsession for the fulfilment of their desires but out of the intelligence that all of us are blessed with!

This was the way out ... the way forward!

I laughed out aloud with heartfelt ecstasy.

*Here was a tool that just got invented based on the case in hand. This powerful tool could help millions of people segregate their fantasies, dreams, aspirations, and goals on the basis of the potential and possibilities in their lives.*

This would enable them to realize their desires and find the path to contentment and clarity.

*I decided to call it The Success Quadrant.*

This would help the Punj family gain clarity of thought, intent, and purpose of each individual life. This would also help to bring the family back together with common desires segregated and acted upon, as the reality remains that people are never in conflict with each other. It is because they are in conflict within themselves and unaware about it that they start feeling that it is others who are stopping them.

I started to examine the Punj House's members' desires within the framework of the Success Quadrant.

# 13

# THE PUNJ FAMILY— DESIRES & THE CONTEMPLATION FOR SUCCESS QUADRANT

## 1. The family living together under one roof: Fantasy

Possibility: Low

When people have varied desires and dreams to follow, life takes them to places. The Punj family needs to choose between being physically together and emotionally & mentally away or the other way.

This is not a possibility they had explored in the first place. It functions in conflict with other possibilities that they need to explore. The external situations, peer-pressures, education, self-expression, social needs were a complex mix which was not in any one person's control. People with great potential and abilities cannot be forced into sanctuaries.

Potential: Low

Under such compulsive circumstances, all family members have a very low emotional potential to share love and happiness with each other. This is so because they are not happy within themselves due to unfulfilled potential, and abandoned and suppressed desires.

Senior Punj needed to let go of this Fantasy. It was making him miserable all the time, despite all his accomplishments in life. He felt discouraged to go any further. He considered himself a failure and ended up playing games within his family, making the very people he loved the most suffer. This was not a desire he needed to chase at all.

## 2. The family business remaining debt free: Fantasy

<u>Possibility: Low</u>

The size and breadth of the business is very high. Without debt, the various profit centre heads consider capital to be surplus and have a tendency to overspend. Debt is a cheap source of money. With the business being capital intensive, such high amounts of investments using capital alone can make the business completely unviable. The possibility consequently is very low.

<u>Potential: Low</u>

The current business model is such that the expansions have consumed most financial commitments over the long term. The on-going M&As require large sums of money. The business can be rationalized in the medium term to optimize debt and to enhance profitability. However, the current business models will not permit a debt-free situation.

Senior Punj needs to let go of this Desire. As he will let go of this Desire, he will be less miserable and will in fact focus on things that may mitigate many risks that are possible to be either avoided or hedged.

## 3. Mynah living a meaningful life: Goal

Possibility: Medium

Mynah lives with immense guilt and rejection. Sometimes in life, people make mistakes but if they start holding themselves guilty forever, they start pushing themselves and live in the constant past. They do not let life flow in its normal and natural course. Mynah needs to realize that every day is a new day.

Potential: High

Mynah is an intelligent and capable girl. Through an enhanced clarity of mind, she simply needs to identify her desires by herself, and explore their relevant expressions. She needs to set goals and accomplish them. She needs to break through her illusive sense of life and has the ability to do so.

Then she will blossom like the beautiful flower, which by the very act of blossoming brings a smile to every onlooker.

This is a Desire that must be chased. Specific outcomes may be defined for this along with laying a mutually agreeable path to achieve it. With such outcomes, Mynah and the Punj Family's concerns will reduce significantly. Happiness will return to those relationships where only worry and irritation exist as of now.

## 4. Kshitij overcoming his over-ambition and the need to prove himself: Aspiration.

Possibility: Medium to High

Kshitij is lost in a race to win. What race? And against whom? He probably himself doesn't know that he has an unquenchable thirst for achievement, which is possible for a man of his energy and background. However, he needs to harness his potential in a much more constructive and planned manner.

<u>Potential: Low to Medium</u>

Kshitij could harness his potential by understanding that empires are not built in a day and neither is there a need for hurry. Everything takes planning and adequately appropriate time to happen. He needs to centre within before he starts to express himself at the outset. Else, he will prove to be destructive for the empire that his father has created over his lifetime.

He needs to set long term goals and work towards their fulfilment in an organized, enthusiastic manner but with patience. For someone to overcome the need to prove himself to others, a deep dive within is required. Once this is achieved, the human potential is unleashed. This is not an easy task. This is not even a psychologically driven awareness. To overcome the need to prove and gain approval requires deep realizations.

This Aspiration needs setting of multiple Goals to be set up as a sub-set to Kshitij's Aspiration. As Kshitij will actively accomplish his personal and professional Goals, his over-dependence on others to do his work will reduce. His self-doubts will fade away leading to removal of biases and the air of superiority in which he lives. Mr Punj needs to engage with his son and mentor him.

## 5. Shekhar to accept larger role in business: Goal

<u>Possibility: High</u>

Shekhar needs to look at his strength and understand the possibilities in life. One does not work for money and fame alone. One's work is one's expression and there is no contentment if one does not achieve one's full expression. His external world is full of possibilities for him.

## Potential: High

He needs to understand his potential. It is his immense potential combined with misplaced values that are forcing him to avoid the spotlight. He has become an escapist of sorts. He is hesitant when he is put under the spotlight. His ability to connect with people makes him special. He can cry, laugh and make that much needed connect with people to make them highly productive.

Definitely, this is a Desire to be chased and fulfilment to be created.

## 6. Dhruv to become a giver and a collaborator: Aspiration.

## Possibility: High

I always believe that every human has the possibility of becoming a giver and a collaborator since being appreciated by others is human. Dhruv is a suppressed and sensitive boy. He needs to recognize his aspirations and work towards them. When we ourselves are filled with happiness and love, it overflows and touches others. Dhruv has an amazing possibility to be happy and joyful and make his teammates experience the same. He has the possibility to make Sonam and his daughters experience the joys and successes in life. But he does not explore these possibilities since he has stopped harnessing his own potential. Dhruv, with a turnaround in his life, can become one of the highest achievers in the Punj Family.

## Potential: Low

He needs to work on his skill and attitude level. He needs to learn from life while actively working with a mentor. His potential is locked in his unwilling mode and the refusal to connect and reach out to people. He is unhappy and needs to re-structure himself. He needs to work on himself and get out of his comfort zones and be open to questions and criticisms. He caps his potential by choosing to live in a shell.

Mr Punj & the elders need to give a loving hand to Dhruv instead of bossing him around.

The fulfilment of this Aspiration will help Dhruv and the entire Punj household achieve the bonding and happiness that they are sorely missing.

## 7. Kshrey to be groomed as a successor: Dream

Possibility: Low to Medium

Kshrey is already questioning the significance of all the success that he witnesses around him. Being ignored by his parents, he has already become disillusioned and without major changes around him, he may grow more and more detached and disillusioned.

In order to raise the possibility of him staying connected with life, his parents need to organize themselves and slow down. They need to pay attention to Kshrey and engage with him. Live a life rather than only making a living. Else, they'll miss out on a huge possibility in their life. The possibility of Kshrey becoming a successor majorly depends on factors driving Kshitij, Sugandha, and the rest of the Punj Family.

Potential: High

Kshrey is a sensible, sensitive and grounded young man. Given the right direction, he could innovate the business with his creative abilities but someone needs to look at him and work with him. His potential is very high.

## 8. Sugandha and Ana to get along with each other: Fantasy

<u>Possibility: Low</u>

Both come from completely opposite mind-set and value systems. Though apparently both are homemakers, they have quite an opposite approach and they need their respective spaces for self-expression.

<u>Potential: Low</u>

Both are unwilling to accept and understand each other's ways. Unwillingness makes the easiest of things tough.

A little physical distance and their own spaces will make a huge difference in making the Punj Family a family in its truest sense. There is no point running after fantasies as they distract one from one's goals and aspirations. Fantasies are chased only when goals, aspirations, and dreams are being achieved consistently.

## 9. Senior Punj and Ana living a carefree life: Goal

<u>Possibility: High</u>

They have all the means to make this happen. Mr Punj has to realize that his life has been an amazing journey full of significant successes. Now it is up to the future generations to make it work. It is time that he now sits back and enjoys the ride.

<u>Potential: High</u>

He needs to set goals and plan for succession and allow each family member to do what they are best at, while establishing a structure in the company and pass on the torch.

**10. The business being run with empathy and the Punj family being a people-friendly organization: Aspiration**

<u>Possibility: High</u>

The Punj Empire has all the ingredients available to take on capable people. It is a highly successful enterprise, which is attracting the best talents already. The world of professional leadership opens various options of structuring the organization to meet such goals.

<u>Potential: Low to Medium</u>

A cultural shift is needed. Old ways of controlling people need to give way to collaboration and empathy. Consistent mentoring and conscious application of new thoughts and ideas can bring the necessary change. As each member of Punj family harnesses his/her individual potential, the organizational potential will be unleashed, taking Punj Enterprises to the greatest possible heights.

I had been contemplating for a while now. I realized that the clock had already struck one. As I walked to my bed, thoughts kept coming to me like unstoppable, torrential rain. I was revisiting some of my thoughts.

# 14

# THE PUNJ FAMILY — GOALS, ASPIRATIONS, DREAMS, FANTASIES & THE APPLICATION OF THE SUCCESS QUADRANT

## 1. Goals and Aspirations: GRANDFATHER– SENIOR PUNJ

I had to commend the fact that Senior Punj had used his potential well. He had the vision to look at the immense possibilities for growth around him and had the courage to explore them by stretching his potential. It was a well-travelled journey from Meerut to Madison Square.

People who have courage to explore their possibilities can only utilise their potential. There can be no desire to achieve success if there is no willingness to explore. People like Senior Mr Punj, with a will to explore, have a certain innocence about them. They are not apologetic about the things they do not know of and they don't feel bad about it. They are embarrassed about what they know of and do not make a display of their skills or achievements.

They are deeply curious and like to explore various options. They have the power of choice. Potential is directly proportionate to the willingness to explore. When I look at Senior Mr Punj, he exemplifies this.

Thus, in the case of business expansion for Senior Mr Punj, he stretched his potential and expanded the possibilities, enabling himself to convert dreams into goals, and achieved success in business. However, he has hit a wall now, as he has been unable to empower his people, who feel at a loss when it comes to decision making due to Mr Punj slowly phasing out of active business engagement. He failed to enable his people to harness their own potential.

He needs to detach himself from the business slowly and leave a legacy in terms of structured succession planning and share values he has built the Punj Empire upon. This could be his immediate goal.

He needs to overcome his conditioned approach and learn how to collaborate with people instead of just being a charismatic leader, a hero.

## 2. Dreams and Fantasies: A Dreamer stretching into Fantasy – KSHITIJ PUNJ

Whenever someone is extremely ambitious, one must check if ambition is rooted in ability or in self-doubt. The only way to know this is whether power and position are making the person heady or humble. When there is a need to prove, more position and power will lead to aggression and domination at times leading to abuse of power too.

Such a situation springs from the emotionally fragile situation of self-doubt or poor self-worth. This hampers the use of self-potential. Such people dream or fantasize a lot. If they have money and power, then they will create outlandish projects and always wish to be Number 1.

This is what Kshitij has. As Kshitij realizes this about

himself, and his engagement with his father, wife and son improves, he will see himself in a completely new light. He will show gratitude to the people who work for him. He will become a collaborator and be more inclusive. He will no longer have the need for any Number 1 slot.

Are dreams wrong? Shall we stop dreaming? Again, there is no way that this will happen. As long as one is alive and the senses are active, one receives data and the brain processes this data. Dreams will happen but when our dreams are laden with doubts, they become the cause of our misery.

If we focus on the achievement of goals and aspirations, then we keep getting motivated with the results that come our way. These keep us hopeful and hope supports faith. With this hope and faith, we nurture our dreams and they come true.

Those who start fulfilling their dreams also start dreaming about the fulfilment of fantasies. Eventually these come true too! Fantasies lead to innovations and we are living in a world full of innovations. This is proof enough that fantasies do come true. It's just that there is a system to its fulfilment. Those who are intelligent and aware, fulfil their dreams and fantasies at no cost to their own lives or to the lives of their loved ones. The ones who are not, become obsessed with their fantasies and innovate at the cost of everyone around them. If there is an easier path available, then why not adopt it?

## 3. No Goals, No Aspirations, No Dreams, No Fantasies: SUGANDHA AND DHRUV

Sometimes, we either become so compliant and fearful, or

so competitive that we are not left with any recognizable desire. This is a state of suppressed desire. It is so deeply suppressed that we have rationalized the suppression. We are basically fearful or competitive but our image about ourselves is of a selfless, sacrificial person who is doing all the right things for others.

Sugandha, during an interaction, shared how she always wanted to be a homemaker or a home decorator despite her education in business, which was a result of the over-ambition of her father, who wanted a son instead of two daughters. She said she would rather enjoy creative pursuits in the hospitality business than doing business transactions.

Mergers/acquisitions were keeping her engaged and away from her child as well as other pursuits. She was conditioned into suppressing her identity to please others and meet their expectations. Being an intelligent person she did that and in the process, lost her will to live. This made her unpleasant. She just needs to overcome her "rational" approach and become sensitive to herself. It's only then that her life will become pleasant and her potential will be tapped.

Dhruv was also in the same boat. He was simply doing what was asked of him and was unwilling to take greater initiatives. He knew Kshitij would put him down in such situations. He was not chasing his desires at all and had become isolated, aloof and unpleasant.

If Kshitij would allow his brother Dhruv to be a part of the business transactions, Sugandha could transform her aspirations into goals. This would also reduce the stress between Sugandha and Dhruv, easing out any outlet for clash of business interests.

## 4. Only Goals, Low Aspirations: SHEKHAR PUNJ

Shekhar was an explorer but an escapist. He was a sensitive achiever who was goal-oriented and had large dreams, but his aspirations were low. He was not exploring his potential and had chosen mediocrity in life. This was making him unhappy but he was aware of this and that was his strength.

Innovation happens when we have the power to think beyond what is within our capacity. That is why it is so important to distance ourselves from our immediate goals sometimes to explore these possibilities. We make those goals our life otherwise and miss out on all the wonderful opportunities waiting in the realm of the unforeseen future. People who do not work on converting their dreams into aspirations and then turn them into goals get into the comfort zone of the known.

Given Shekhar's affinity to India and the Indian culture, he needs to move to India and head the Punj's interests in the Asia-Pacific Region. That region is suffering due to poor offshore management. With effective mentoring and coaching, he shall be able to come into his own as a leader, no longer remaining a follower.

I made a mental note of areas to work on for his mentoring program.

## 5. Only Fantasies: Desires different from the rest of the family – MYNAH PUNJ.

She seemed to have been to the hell and back, trying to find her feet and her life's purpose. From childhood, she had been taught to suppress her emotions, leading to clogged emotions and blurred thought processes. Her intrinsic desire was to understand life but she lived in an illusion that renunciation from worldly life would help her attain the purpose of her life.

Understanding life is only possible through engaging with life. She needs to have clarity of her desire and purpose. She needs to understand her own emotional cycle and the emotions of others around her. She needs to be empathetic rather than being sympathetic towards people.

I see immense potential in her to manage operations of the US hospitality business with her qualification and desire to help people. She can learn to be truly meditative and help others through her people-management skills. In hotel operations, she would have opportunities to interact with people from all walks of life and gain new insights. Once immersed in work, she would learn the true meaning of meditation, with her eyes open.

*

I closed my diary and sat in absolute silence for a few minutes, closing all the thoughts and reflections, with only the faint cooing of a night bird being a distant intrusion between silence and subsequent contemplation.

I opened my eyes, looked into the mirror in the room and found a child-like smile pasted on my face. Coming back to bed, I offered my prayers and gratitude, called it a night, and slept like a baby.

# 15

# THE MORNING

Each day as we wake up, we are more than who we were yesterday. Through awareness, we explore more of who we are and make more of who we can be. The Success Quadrant teaches us the how of doing this.

A fundamental conflict of desires, both my own and of others, if it is laid to rest, can resolve a million conflicts. This is the first step. It is this morning that brings that drop of dew, a freshness propelling us to move ahead.

My discussions with each member of the family, both in person and collectively, had resulted in their realisations. There was no point in me having answers for them.

What is important is for the seeker to be able to find his/her own answers. It had not been easy either for them or for me. For people to undo what has been justified for years cannot be simple. Yet, the upbringing of each member had something very humble and innocent. They were resistant, but also uniquely receptive! They had sharp minds and as they sat with me, they easily tore themselves apart and I knew that they would just as easily rebuild themselves in no time.

Death is important for life. With each realisation, something within them died as their visions gave them a rebirth. There was a blossoming of minds and of spirit. The horizon was suddenly clearer and brighter. They wanted to reach out to themselves and the ones they loved and cared for so deeply. True bonds of freedom had set in. Love was now combined with genuine respect for oneself and for each other.

As they embraced their desires, they had started setting and working on their goals and aspirations already. This is the joy of working with people, for once triggered, their intelligence simply takes over and they become more human…

The weeklong stay at the Punj Home had come to an end. My bags were packed and I was ready to leave. I had switched off the public alarm system and the residents of each floor were invited to come for breakfast together. Each chair on the dining table was occupied and we all said an invocation together before indulging in a simple Indian breakfast that Ana had prepared for us. She looked at each family member present on the table and offered her gratitude to me with folded hands.

As I poured out my contemplative heart and soul, I felt deeply for the family.

*Sometimes, we are unable to recognize the wonderful blessings bestowed on us by the Grace and simply while away the precious gifts given to us by life.*

A family so capable should rise to unprecedented levels and shine so bright that everyone looks up to them.

A clear understanding of the self and each other's desires had replaced hesitation and scepticism. They not only felt humbled but also had a new energy, a new enthusiasm. Clouds of confusion had given way to clarity. Their conduct had changed. They had changed. There was a talk of collaboration, of engagement, of support. There was willingness and cheer since each one knew how to fulfil his or her personal desires while fulfilling others' needs.

They felt powerful. It was one team. It was one family. Clarity was truly liberating!

This clarity of desires provides an insight into our dreams, which are also our vision. Decision-making becomes easy since goals and aspirations are chosen in line with dreams and vision.

Constant focus on goals produces consistent results. Such results provide the necessary impetus and encouragement to constantly stretch into the aspirations by improving personal and collective potential through better use of body, mind and emotions.

As goals and aspirations are met, hope starts replacing doubt and produces faith, that in turn leads to creating possibilities where none existed earlier. Grace starts to play its role. Dreams and visions come true!

*Now is the time for innovation!*
*Let us fulfil our fantasies too!*
*Who says Divinity can't be explored!*

# EPILOGUE— CONFLICT

I had requested for an unaccompanied drive to the airport and all the family members stood with folded hands in the driveway as I approached the limousine. Kshrey walked further with me and held my hand. He had met me for a morning walk earlier. When I descended from the guest room, he was already waiting for me in the garden with his walking shoes on. He was a highly observant boy and was full of questions.

"Does it all end here?" he asked, raising a question during our morning walk towards the Central Park. I had nodded my head.

"Does it end at all? Ever?" he had asked again. "How many times do we have to keep going back and forth to understand what we desire and what quadrant it falls in at that point in life?"

I had kept quiet as usual. He was willing to find answers and who was I to lead him?

"Do you think I am a misfit in this society? I feel I am so different from the rest!"

I could feel his angst. "Whatever we imagine is a possibility waiting to be achieved, Kshrey. There is a way to live and participate with life in a way that makes us Divine," I assured him.

I rested my hand on his shoulder and said, "We say desires are endless but it is the conflicts within that make them seem so distant. We say that opportunities knock our door, and we keep waiting for that knock. They are always there, waiting for us to knock their doors. When in conflict, we look up to the learned and knowledgeable to guide us but who can guide us on our intrinsic desires? Who can show us the right path? This is where the journey begins."

I owed him one more answer before I left him with all the empowering questions raised between us. "You asked me in the morning if you were a misfit in the society? I say, aren't we all misfits in the society? That doesn't bother me. It is important not to become a misfit with one's own life, while societies take care of themselves! Remember that, Kshrey, and always stay in touch with yourself."

*This journey was coming to an end. A new journey was slated to begin.*

I smiled at him and got into the car. I had intended to halt at the Central Park briefly before heading to the airport, to savour the sight of pale pink flower clusters and marvel at the beauty of the Divine. Cherries had blossomed on Yoshino cherry trees the previous night and I could feel them calling out to me since morning. That was one among the many calls that needed my urgent attention.

Upon my departure from New York, I waved goodbye to one story and eagerly waited to hear more of them, for each story is unique and there is nothing that cannot be solved by one's own design. Therein manifests the potential to possibility transformation.

**Introduction to the Punj Family:**

The Punj Family can be anywhere around you. Maybe it is you. This is a family that is, like any family, living together, yet trying to find its identity and purpose. The surname tries to outweigh the individual. Family ambitions capture both attention and imagination. An entire world exists within the confines of a house and a family. All emotions play to their full volumes. A heady mix where each member should wish well for others yet ends up competing and taking others for granted, and where being accepted remains an aspiration and criticism prevails over providing support.

Each member of the family is unique in his/her aspirations and identity. In spite of setting common values, same set of parents, same teachings, same conditioning, the character of each family member differs. Parents keep trying to keep everyone together unsuccessfully. It really is that family which we meet everyday... yours and mine.

While characters and situations are fictionalised, emotions are not. A narrative is chosen to function as a vehicle to communicate an idea, which when contemplated, leads to self-realisations.

It is not a work of fiction. It is not even a work of reality. It is somewhere in-between.

The work we do with people is intense, complex and deep. Our goal is to shed off intensity, complexity, and fill the depth. Our aim is truth. Our purpose is evolution. Our subject is the self. Our object of study is also the self.

This book is a part of the series of giving an insight into the kind of work we offer. A kind of Possibility there is.

There is a total of 7 more parts planned to this extended series. Each of the writings will offer an insight into each character of the Punj family and his/her joys and sorrows, pains and ecstasies, highlighting his/her personal journey to the centre of his/her self, in his/her own unique way. These 7 characters represent the 7 notes of the music, the 7 colours of the rainbow and the 7 chakras of the human system. These 7 characters offer 7 unique paths to liberation, the 7 vital steps to evolution. They revolve around the original theory of human evolution through 7 steps leading to the eighth step — the Ashtapada*!

It is easy to write, much easier to read but difficult to apply. It is much more difficult to steer application. Keeping this in mind, each book will offer some very practical tools for application. As you use these tools, apply them in your life; you will get your self-realisations. Believe them to be true.

As you grow in your insights, you will witness growth around you.


Love,

Shalini and Sameer

# GLOSSARY:

Many Hindi or Sanskrit words have been used. This glossary will help you understand the deeper meanings of the text written and presented to you. Each name conveys a context and meaning attached.

## Glossary of Vernacular Terms

- Sugandha - fragrance.

- Prem - love.

- Prakash - light.

- Folded hands - a formal gesture of greeting in the Indian sub-continent.

- Yoga - a system of practices that enable holistic, physical, mental and spiritual wellbeing.

- Trishul – trident.

- Kailash Manasarovar - a place nestled in the snow-clad Trans-Himalayan Range located in the Tibetan Plateau, considered to be of highest spiritual and religious importance.

- Bhaiya - endearing way of referring to one's elder brother.

- Ji - When the term 'Ji' is attached as a suffix to one's name, it expresses respect and acknowledgement of one's seniority (in age/profession/knowledge/ intellect) over the other.

- Meerut - a city located in Northern India.

- New Delhi - the capital of India.

- Namaste - a traditional Indian greeting or gesture of

respect, made by bringing the palms together before the face or chest and bowing.

- Annapurna - The 'One' who gives people food and nourishment; Annapurna is also the name of a Goddess, worshipped in India.

- Feng Shui - a system of laws, devised by ancient Chinese philosophers, considered to govern spatial arrangement and orientation in relation to the flow of energy (chi), and whose favourable or unfavourable effects are taken into account when siting and designing buildings and decorating the interiors of buildings.

- Holi - the Indian festival of colours.

- Diwali - the Indian festival of lights that celebrates the triumph of Good (symbolized by light) over Evil (symbolized by darkness).

- Ravana - Ravana, a demon King, was said to have ruled Lanka (present-day Sri Lanka), according to the Indian text, Ramayana. Ravana is portrayed as an educated, informed, knowledgeable yet lustful, powerful and evil man, who abducted Sita, the wife of the protagonist and God Rama.

- Ram - A common household name kept after Lord Rama.

- Beta - an endearing way of referring to one's son.

- Hindi - an Indian language, predominantly spoken by people living in the Northern region of India.

- Ashtapada - an 8x8 board game played in ancient India, which predates chess. It is also referred to as the "Eighth Step". It also refers to the Mountain ranges in the Kailash Region in the Trans Himalayan Tibetan Plateau.

# ABOUT THE AUTHORS

## SHALINI KAMBOJ
### *Co-Founder and CEO at SKC World*

A Mentor, Guide, Coach, Psychologist, Author and the CEO i.e. The Chief Emotions Officer of SKC.World. At her core she is a very conscious and spiritual person. She is an expert in Transactional Analysis, analysing organizational problems and providing implementable grounded & practical solutions. She has over two decades of experience, working with Sameer, her husband, as mentors to 1000s of entrepreneurs, promoters of corporate houses, and C-Level Professionals of various small, medium and large companies of varied industries. She helps people become conscious entrepreneurs.

## SAMEER KAMBOJ
### *Conscious Entrepreneur, Co-Founder at SKC World*

Mentor, Guide, Coach, Consultant, Musician, a 'Master in Gyan-Yoga'. The founder of SKC.World, a company that aims to plant the seed of consciousness in entrepreneurship. Sameer is on a mission to "touch a million lives". He stands as an example, that one can live life consciously a moment at a time, and through the "Ancient Indian Science of Gyan-Yoga", he helps people become conscious in everything they do. He profoundly calls it "Applied Spirituality". He is a Speaker at various events on entrepreneurship, management and also runs a blog on his website www.sameerkamboj.com.

On our way, to touch a Million Lives...

## MORE POSSIBILITIES TO ENGAGE

Shalini and Sameer are co-founder of SKC World, a company on a mission to create an era of conscious entrepreneurship that enables and helps people master the science of scaling up and success in their businesses and life Joyfully. SKC does this through:

1. **Consulting** services for scaling up of organisations.

2. Different **mentoring & coaching** programs to develop people and organisations to gain greater scale of success and joy in life through inner transformation and state of the art work skills.

3. **Compliance** to ensure regular monitoring of processes, implementation of them to remove complications and build platform for scaling up.

SKC World has helped 1000+ entrepreneurs, business owners and C-level professionals achieve Success and scale with joy and become conscious entrepreneurs.

To know more visit: www.skc.world

# THE POSSIBILITIES OF POTENTIAL
## BY SHALINI AND SAMEER KAMBOJ


# WORKBOOK

# Step 1: My Desires

## List down any and all your Desires.

*Note: At this point, do not worry about whether your desires seem viable or non-viable; possible or impossible; big or small, realistic or unrealistic; silly or overambitious. Just write down whatever comes to the mind.*

# Step 2: The Success Quadrant

<u>Now that you have listed down all your desires, analyze and place each desire into the appropriate quadrant.</u>

*Note: Remember, POSSIBILITIES are that which are external to us; POTENTIAL is what is internal to us.*

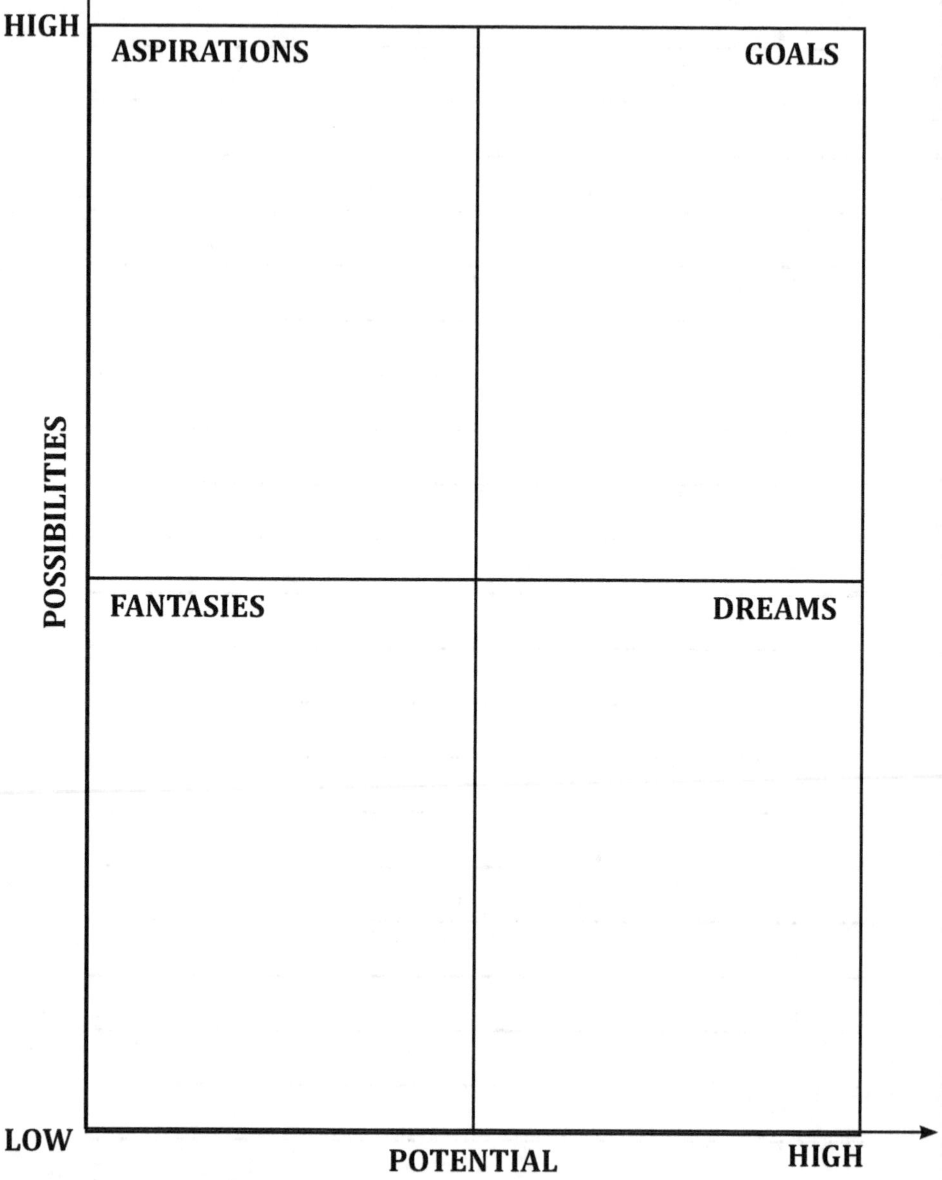

HIGH

| ASPIRATIONS | GOALS |
|---|---|
| FANTASIES | DREAMS |

POSSIBILITIES

LOW     POTENTIAL     HIGH

# Step 2: The Success Quadrant (cont.)

# Step 3: Transform your Desires into Goals!

1.  <u>Convert all your Desires in the "Goals Quadrant" into Short Term Goals/Long Term Goals</u>

2.  <u>Convert all your Desires in the "Aspirations Quadrant" into Long Term Goals</u>

*Note: Do remember to set target dates for every goal.*

**<u>Short Term Goals</u>**

| S. No. | Short Term Goals | Start Date | Target Date | Finish Date |
|--------|------------------|------------|-------------|-------------|
|        |                  |            |             |             |

# Short Term Goals (cont.)

| S. No. | Short Term Goals | Start Date | Target Date | Finish Date |
|---|---|---|---|---|
|  |  |  |  |  |
| S. No. | Short Term Goals | Start Date | Target Date | Finish Date |

# Long Term Goals

| S. No. | Long Term Goals | Start Date | Target Date | Finish Date |
|---|---|---|---|---|
|  |  |  |  |  |

## Long Term Goals (cont.)

| S. No. | Long Term Goals | Start Date | Target Date | Finish Date |
|---|---|---|---|---|
|  |  |  |  |  |

"Being divine is a possibility,

Exploration any lesser is mediocrity"


Sameer Kamboj

# NOTES

# Notes

# Notes

# Notes

# Notes

# Notes

# Notes

# Notes

# Notes

# Notes

# Notes

# Notes

# Notes

# Notes

# Notes

# Notes

# Notes

# Notes

# Notes

# Notes

# Notes

# Notes

# Notes

# REDISCOVERY

## *of*

## VEDIC AND ANCIENT BHARAT

Canvas of India's Mathematics, Science, Astronomy,
Yoga, Literature and Architecture (1500 BCE to 1000 CE)


**Ankan Bhaduri**

Programmer Analyst
Cognizant Technology Solutions, Kolkata, India

**Dr. Anirban Das**

Professor & Vice President- Innovation Council, University of
Engineering and Management, Kolkata, India
Innovation Ambassador, Ministry of Education, AICTE, India
Visiting Scientist, University of Malaya, Malaysia
Inclusive Policy Lab Expert, UNESCO, USA
Honorary Vice President- EURASIA Research, USA Honorary Scientist,
BrainHealthTech NeuroLabs International

ISBN 979-8-89186-957-8